HAPPY
BIRTHDAYS

HAPPY
BIRTHDAYS

How to decorate birthday cakes, tables and gifts – for people who think they can't

ROBINSON & SCHOFIELD

BLOOMSBURY

First published 1990

Copyright © 1990 by Greg Robinson and Max Schofield
Bloomsbury Publishing Limited, 2 Soho Square, London W1V 5DE

British Library Cataloguing in
Publication Data

A CIP record for this
book is available
from the
British Library

ISBN 0 7475 0633 7

Colour separations by Fotographics Limited, London and Hong Kong
Printed in Great Britain by Butler and Tanner Ltd, Frome and London

HAPPY BIRTHDAYS
was produced by Nigel Osborne
115J Cleveland Street, London W1

Art Direction	Nigel Osborne
Editor	Judy Martin
Design	Sally Stockwell
Photography	Matthew Chattle

CHAPTER 1

GETTING STARTED

Giving a birthday party, or for that matter any kind of party, can tax even the most creative imagination with the effort to produce something out of the ordinary. The birthday cake can pose a problem, not because spectacular cakes are necessarily difficult to make in themselves, but because new ideas can be hard to find. You may go out to buy cards, wrappings and party decorations and come home with something that was not quite what you had in mind, either through indecision or lack of choice. So how do you go about creating that special atmosphere for a birthday party that does not take forever to organize or cost the earth, but that is different and unique.

Happy Birthdays is a collection of new and exciting ideas to stimulate your imagination and show you how even the smallest details can make all the difference to your celebration. Whether your party is designed around the zodiac sign or the season of the year in which the birthday falls, or a special interest that the birthday person may have, we offer a whole host of brilliant ideas that you can copy exactly or feel free to interpret in your own way.

CREATING THE PARTY MOOD

We present more than 30 designs for the all-important birthday cake, using edible and non-edible components to create eye-catching and unusual decorative effects. The detailed instructions for each cake introduce a range of decorating techniques, some of which you may never have tried, but all of which are easier than they look and a source of endless creative potential.

As well as a fantastic range of cakes, we have included lots of ideas for extra items that contribute to the whole atmosphere of the party. These range from hand-made gifts and wrappings to special lighting effects, from delicious desserts and party treats to hanging decorations and beautifully sculptured table centres. Throughout the emphasis is on finding an inventive approach to your theme using simple methods and a wide range of readily available materials. You do not have to be an expert in any particular field to produce something exceptional and memorable – candlelight transformed into pale glowing lilies, a salad served in a glistening coloured ice bowl, a table centre made from beautiful breads or fruits.

We have provided clear instructions for recreating every one of the items on display in the following pages, including many delicious recipes as well as step-by-step guidance on making the decorations and suggestions for alternative methods for achieving particular effects. But we hope these details will also encourage you to take a fresh look at your own skills, talents and resources and to interpret the projects in ways that give your party celebrations your own uniquely individual touch.

CAKES AND ICING

As the centrepiece of the birthday party, the cake should both look beautiful and taste delicious. The type of cake you choose can vary as long as it is suitable for the type of decoration, as described below, and in some cases the ingredients and texture of the cake can be chosen entirely to suit your personal taste or the preferences of your party guests. With the icing it is not quite so simple, as the different types of icing are appropriate to particular purposes and effects. Sometimes the icing is merely a smooth covering for the cake and all the decoration is added over the icing layer; in other instances the icing actually creates a sculpted or textured effect essential to the look of the finished cake. Here we explain the few general points you need to know about cakes and icing, and provide the basic recipes.

THE CAKE

Many of our birthday cake designs can be adapted to whatever kind of cake you wish to serve. Decoration for the Aries and Capricorn birthday cakes, for example, does not actually touch the cake: for Virgo and Scorpio, the decoration is designed as an icing plaque that sits on top of the cake. For these you could choose to use a sponge, fruit cake, chocolate or ginger cake – anything according to your taste.

There are two general points you should bear in mind. If the cake is carrying any weight of iced or non-edible decoration, it needs to be firm enough to retain its shape before and after decorating. If the cake itself is to be sculpted to form the basic shape of the design, you need to choose cake with a fine, even texture that will not crumble or fragment as you carve it with a knife. A firm madeira cake is ideal.

Most cakes will rise during cooking to form a slightly domed top. We usually cut off the dome to give a firm, flat surface for the decoration, although this is of course not essential in the designs where the cake is entirely hidden within the decoration. An exception is rich fruit cake. We turn this upside down on a cake board, so that the bottom becomes a flat top, and fill the gap between cake and board with marzipan.

For many of the designs, you can adapt the size of the cake to suit your own requirements. We have usually provided details of the size and shape of the cake used in each of our demonstrations, as this provides a useful guideline for quantities and relative proportions when it comes to marzipanning, icing and decorating. You can if you choose follow our instructions to the letter, but you can equally calculate what you will need for a smaller or larger cake, according to the number of party guests you wish to serve. Certain designs may lose impact if made smaller, such as the seasonal tiered cakes on pages 66-73, which do look best if they are rather large and lavish. There may also be some practical considerations, such as for the Leaping Fish cake designed for the Pisces birthday (page 63), which is quite heavily sculpted and might be difficult to handle on a smaller scale.

Remember to plan for extra baking time if the design requires more than one cake. Each cake should be baked separately in the centre of the oven at the correct temperature.

We have included here three basic recipes that provide different tastes and textures. You will find other useful recipes throughout the book, including a chocolate truffle mix that needs no baking and is ideal for cakes made in moulds, and a delicious sponge and meringue cake (see the Summer Strawberry Cake on page 75) that is very decorative in itself.

BASIC KITCHEN EQUIPMENT

cake tins
cooling rack
large mixing bowl
rolling pin
wooden spoons
whisk
sieve
pastry brush
spatula
large, sharp kitchen knife (for carving cake)
decorative cutters and moulds

MARZIPAN

Marzipan – almond paste – adds a delicious taste to the cake, but the main reason for covering a cake with marzipan before icing it is more practical. The marzipan seals the cake, keeping the moisture in, and provides a firm, dry base for the icing layer. It is important that the icing is not in contact with a moist surface.

Marzipan handles like pastry. It should be kept at room temperature, when it will roll out easily. To fix marzipan to the surface of the cake, an adhesive layer of apricot jam is used, usually sieved to remove the pieces of skin and fruit. The jam is applied thinly and evenly.

As a basic covering for the cake, the marzipan is rolled out to a sheet about $1/4$in (6mm) thick. Aim to achieve a smooth, flat surface when marzipanning a cake, as any irregularities will tend to show up in the icing layers. In a number of the designs we have also used marzipan to model a sculpted section on top of the cake or additional detail that goes with other iced decoration.

You can colour marzipan, which is yellow or white in its natural form, by adding food colour and working it through until the whole amount of marzipan is evenly coloured.

ICING

We have used three main kinds of icing throughout the projects in this book. It is important to use the type of icing recommended in the instructions for a particular cake, as each icing has its own characteristics and is used for a particular purpose. The ingredients of all three are inexpensive, so if you are unused to handling icing it is worth making up a batch of each kind and experimenting with them before you start work on a specific project.

Fondant Icing

Fondant icing produces a smooth, soft finish that is easy to cut. It can be rolled out into a pliable sheet that moulds itself easily to sculptural detail on a cake. We have used it as the final layer before adding colour decoration in many of the projects for the zodiac and themed birthday cakes.

With practice, it is easy to handle but there are two points to watch out for. One is that fondant icing reproduces detail very accurately, so it will also reflect any imperfections in the marzipanning of the cake. The second is that it remains soft for several hours after application and even light fingertip pressure will mark it. If air bubbles appear in the icing, you can simply prick them with a pin to let out the air.

You can store unused fondant icing by wrapping it in plastic film. If it feels a little dry when you roll it out, moisten the icing with a few drops of water and knead it until it is soft and pliable again.

FONDANT ICING

18oz (500g)/4 cups icing sugar
1 egg white
2 tbsp (30ml)/¹/₈ cup liquid glucose
cornflour

Put the icing sugar, egg white and liquid glucose into a bowl. Mix with a wooden spoon until the mixture resembles lumps of breadcrumbs. Knead until the mixture takes on the consistency of bread dough. Add a little cornflour as necessary to prevent the mixture from becoming too sticky. The icing is ready when it no longer feels sticky and can be rolled out on a work surface lightly dusted with cornflour without sticking. You can use it straight away or leave it overnight wrapped in plastic film and stored in an airtight container.

Gelatin Icing

Gelatin icing is used for carved and moulded decoration. It has a wonderful elasticity and can be rolled out or shaped by hand, but it dries hard and is difficult to cut as compared to fondant icing. For this reason it is used decoratively rather than as a cake covering. We have used it in a variety of ways in the cake designs – for example, to mould the lion's head for the Leo cake (page 34), to form a freestanding dome over the Capricorn cake (page 59), to model flowers and leaves as decoration for the Spring and Autumn cakes (pages 66 and 70), and to create beautiful drapery for our Madame Butterfly figure (page 110).

GELATIN ICING

18oz (500g)/4 cups icing sugar
¹/₂oz (12.5g) gelatin powder
4 tbsp (60ml)/¹/₄ cup water
2 tsp (10ml) liquid glucose
cornflour

Put the water in a heatproof bowl and add the gelatin powder. Leave to soak for 2 minutes. Place the bowl in a pan with ¹/₂in (1.2cm) water and set on the stove. Heat gently until the gelatin dissolves. Remove from the heat and stir in the liquid glucose. Allow to cool for 2 minutes. Turn the mixture into a bowl containing the icing sugar and mix together. If the mixture seems wet add some cornflour, sufficient so that the icing can be worked like bread dough and leaves the sides of the bowl clean. The finished icing should not be sticky to the touch. Wrap in plastic film and place in an airtight container until ready to use.
The icing dries in contact with the air. If left unwrapped, a crust forms. If this happens, cut off the dried crust and wrap what remains in film. If the icing firms up, knead until soft before using.

Royal Icing

Royal icing was at one time more commonly used as a cake covering, but it is extremely hard and brittle to cut so fondant icing is often preferred. Royal icing has a paste-like quality that is easy to manipulate and it sets quickly, so it is ideal for certain effects such as the rough "plaster" background for the painted fragment on the Aquarian cake (page 58) and to represent churned snow in our humorous representation of a skier who has crashed into a snowdrift (page 74). It is also used for piping, as in the Virgo cameo (page 38). The consistency can be altered for different purposes by using more egg white, as recommended in the instructions for the cakes where appropriate. Finally, royal icing makes an excellent, and very strong, edible glue that can be used to attach iced or non-edible decorations to the cake.

ROYAL ICING

1 egg white
12oz (350g) icing sugar, sifted

Beat the egg white to break it up and add the icing sugar in batches, mixing after each addition. Add sufficient icing sugar to make the required consistency. If not required immediately, cover the icing with plastic film, pressing down gently to remove air bubbles. Do not store the icing in the refrigerator, as it will absorb moisture that will alter the consistency.

MADEIRA CAKE

8oz (225g) butter or margarine
8oz (225g)/1 cup caster sugar
4 eggs
8oz (225g)/1¹/₂ cups self-raising flour
4oz (125g)/³/₄ cup plain flour

Cream the butter or margarine and sugar together until light and fluffy. Add the eggs one at a time and beat into the mixture, adding a spoonful of flour to the mixture after each egg and beating again. Sift the remaining flours together and fold into the creamed mixture. Turn the mixture into a greased and lined 8in (20cm) round tin and level the top. Bake in a preheated oven at 325°F (160°C)/gas mark 3 for 1 hour 25 minutes, until the cake is well risen and firm to the touch. Leave for 5-10 minutes, then turn out onto a wire rack to cool.

RICH FRUIT CAKE

2lb 6oz (1kg) mixed dried fruit
5oz (150g) glacé cherries
4oz (125g) mixed peel, chopped
4oz (125g) ground almonds
1¹/₂ tsp ground cinnamon
1 tsp ground mixed spice
14oz (400g)/2⁵/₈ cups plain flour
12oz (350g) butter or margarine
12oz (350g)/1¹/₂ cups light brown sugar
6 eggs
brandy or whisky

Grease a 10in (25cm) cake tin and line with a double layer of waxed paper. Mix together the dried fruit, quartered cherries and mixed peel, in a bowl or plastic bag. Add the almonds, spices and half the flour. Mix the ingredients in the bowl or toss in the plastic bag to coat the fruit with flour, spice and almonds. Cream the butter or margarine with sugar until light and fluffy. Do not overbeat, or the cake will be heavy. Add the eggs one or two at a time and mix well, adding a tablespoon of flour after each egg. Fold in any remaining flour and then add the dried fruit mixture. Spread the mixture in the tin and level off the top. Tie two or three thicknesses of brown paper or newspaper around the tin and bake in a pre-heated oven at 300°F (150°C)/gas mark 2 for 3³/₄ hours. Check after half the cooking time and if necessary, turn down the heat to 275°F (140°C)/gas mark 1 and cover the tin with a double layer of paper or cooking foil to prevent overcooking on the surface. To test for readiness, insert a skewer into the centre of the cake. If done, the skewer will come out clean. Allow the cake to cool in the tin. Turn the cake out of the tin and prick the surface all over with a skewer. Spoon brandy or whisky over the cake and wrap in a double thickness of waxed paper and cooking foil. The cake can be allowed to mature over a period from three weeks to a few months, and the "feeding" with brandy or whisky can be repeated at intervals over this period.

9

COLOURFUL CAKES

Colour is one of the most vital decorative elements and in our birthday cake designs we have used food colours in a variety of ways. A beautifully simple form of decoration is a picture painted on a plaque of firm icing. For the Taurean, this becomes a personalized sign (page 22). In the Aquarian cake (page 58) the plaque appears as a painted fragment from an ancient mural. Our alternative design for Aquarius (page 59) is a beautiful stone-like effect created with rich shades of blue and purple.

Where carving and modelling are used to give three-dimensional form to the cake, colour work enhances the shape and adds decorative detail. A simple example is the Cancer crab cake (page 30) where the colour is ornamental rather than realistic but helps to define the emerging crab against its background. Perhaps the most vivid and elaborate use of colour in association with modelling is our dramatic figure of Madame Butterfly (page 110).

Painting on an iced surface is by no means the only way to use food colours. Throughout the book you will find other applications, such as the colourful marzipan hexagons of our simple but stylish fan cake (page 78) and the beautiful Virgo cameo of coloured icing (page 38).

Paint effects *(top to bottom) Gradated tones; blended colours; stippling; dragged and stippled colour; sponging; potato cuts.*

11

CAKE DECORATION

On these pages we describe the basic materials and techniques that are used in projects throughout the book. Many of the skills you acquire in decorating the cake are equally applicable to your approach to preparing table decorations, wrappings and gift items, and the general stock of materials and equipment recommended is useful for making party decorations of all kinds. If you are a newcomer to cake decorating, you will discover that a small repertoire of techniques in painting with food colours gives you a surprising amount of versatility. As for the apparently more elaborate forms of ornamentation, whether these involve cutting and shaping icing decoration or using everyday materials such as paper and card, you will again find that a surprisingly effective result can be achieved by quite simple means.

APPLYING FOOD COLOURS

There is a wide range of food colours available from specialist shops stocking cake making and decorating materials. As you can see from the variety of effects illustrated throughout this book, you can achieve many shades of colour, from palest pastel tints to brilliant primary colours to solid black. In some cases we have recommended that you use food paste colours, which are of thick consistency and produce strong colour effects even when worked into marzipan or icing. You can also obtain food colour pens which are similar to ordinary fibre-tip pens or markers. These can make it easier to draw fine detail, especially on a curving surface.

Gold and silver food colours make an important contribution to the decorative effects of several of our designs. Edible metallic lustre powder sometimes provides the perfect finishing touch, as in our Pisces birthday cake (page 63) where silver lustre powder gives an added shimmer to the fish bodies. However, these products do have a slightly metallic taste and it is best not to use them in great quantity.

Painting techniques

Food colours behave in much the same way as ordinary water-based paints, in that you can mix and blend them to produce different hues and tones, or paint one colour over another when the first has dried. By diluting a colour with increasing amounts of water you can produce a range of tones – brilliant red lightening gradually to pale pink, for example. When working on a raised or curved surface, be careful not to make the colour too wet or it will run over the cake where it is not intended to go.

By mixing and blending colours when they are still wet you can achieve a subtle gradation of hues, from yellow through orange to red, for example, or green merging into blue. Textured surfaces and effects of broken colour can be achieved by stippling and dragging techniques. Stippling can be done either by dabbing the tip of a fine brush repeatedly over the surface or by splaying the bristles of a large brush and dabbing them gently over the surface (see the third and fourth inset pictures on the previous page). You can build up mixed hues and tones by stippling two or more colours together. Dragging or drybrush technique makes a striated texture that can resemble wood grain or, as in the lion's head cake on page 35, animal fur. The brush is loaded with colour, then blotted to remove the excess, and you then drag the bristles over the surface to leave broken lines of colour.

Applicators

If you intend to use much painted decoration, it is worth investing in good quality paintbrushes as cheap ones are likely to shed hairs that will spoil the paint finish. Sable hair or high quality synthetic hair brushes of the type used for watercolour work are readily available from artists' suppliers and some stationers, in a range of sizes. Round hair brushes that make a good point are the most versatile.

Sponges are very useful for applying large areas of blended or textured colour. Different effects are obtained depending on the texture of the sponge, varying from coarse, open textures that create a mottled paint finish to very fine, close-textured sponges that can be used to achieve areas of solid, flat colour.

For some of the subtler effects of gradated colour, as in the Capricorn dome (page 54), we used an airbrush to apply the colour as a fine spray that produces a flawless finish. An airbrush is a specialized and relatively expensive item of equipment, but you can obtain similar effects using an ordinary mist-sprayer of the type used to spray plants. The colour needs to be completely smooth and liquid to spray evenly without spattering. Sponging is often a perfectly practical alternative to spraying. If you use a fine sponge and dab on the colour stage by stage, blending one area into the next, you can achieve a smooth finish. For a slightly coarser effect, you can use a toothbrush to spray colour. Load the bristles with colour, then hold the toothbrush over the cake surface and draw your finger back across the bristles so that the colour is thrown off in tiny droplets.

To create pattern effects you can use stencils (see pages 122-126) or even the humble potato cut (see inset picture on the previous page). Simply halve a potato and cut out a raised motif on the cross-section, then dip the motif in colour and press the potato onto the icing surface. If you do something wrong when painting, or the effect does not turn out as you expected, wait for the colour to dry and then paint over it. You can also use the colours to disguise minor faults in the icing layer.

ADAPTING ARTWORK TO SIZE

For each of the cakes in which the decoration consists of a painted symbol or image, we have supplied a drawing of the image that you can use as the basis of

your own design. It will be necessary to enlarge the image, either to the size of the cake as recommended or to fit your own cake if you are making it larger or smaller than the one shown. There are two basic methods of enlarging artwork to a required size.

The first method is to make use of photocopying facilities that may be available at your local print shop or office equipment suppliers. A photocopier can be used to enlarge the image automatically to your specifications, and the service is quite inexpensive.

Alternatively, there is a simple method that you can use to enlarge the image yourself. Trace off the design and draw a square box around it, to fit the outline of the image as tightly as possible. Divide each side of the box into equal proportions and draw a grid of smaller squares over the image. On a separate sheet of paper (you can use greaseproof paper or baking parchment as your tracing paper), draw a square at a size that fits around the image area on your cake. Divide this larger square into a squared grid with exactly the same number of divisions as in the smaller grid. Copy the small design square by square onto the larger grid. You can then use this enlargement as a pattern for tracing down the design on the cake.

Transferring the image

There are two ways of tracing your image down onto the icing surface. A very quick and easy method is to use graphite paper. This is coated on one side with a thin film of graphite, the material used in pencil leads, which when traced over leaves a fine black line on the surface below. To trace off your design all you need do is slip the graphite paper, graphite side down, between your paper pattern and the icing layer and go over the lines of the image. You should only use this method if you do not intend to eat the iced decoration.

To transfer the design without leaving an inedible trace, you can use the point of a cocktail stick to impress the lines of your design on the icing while it is still soft. Place the paper pattern on the icing surface and press lightly with the cocktail stick – you need only leave a faint impression that you can follow when painting with food colours.

MATERIALS AND EQUIPMENT

We have used many different techniques and materials in making the decorations for our birthday and theme cakes. Sometimes we recommend specialist items of equipment, such as a small

sponge roller for applying colour or lino-cutting tools for creating incised decoration. Usually, these items are quite widely available but where possible we have suggested alternatives that may be among your ordinary kitchen equipment – such as a potato peeler as a substitute for lino-cutting gouges.

For cutting, we use a scalpel with disposable blades. This type of knife is equally suitable for cutting icing or paper and cuts icing shapes much more accurately than a kitchen knife. The blades are very fine and sharp, keeping a clean edged cut even on intricate details. Scalpels are readily available from artists' suppliers.

To find the many decorative items included in the designs, we have ranged quite widely. Some of the items are available from the haberdashery counter, some from your local florist or garden centre, others from specialist paper goods suppliers, novelty shops or gift shops. Before you start work on a project, it is advisable to read through the list of ingredients and material provided with each project, and the instructions for making the decoration, so that you can see what materials you may have to hand and what you will need to buy.

Of course, simple items such as ribbons and cord can be easily obtained and you can often vary such aspects as the width and colour of ribbon decoration according to your own preferences. There is no need to follow the design as shown in every detail. For specialist items that may prove more elusive, especially if you do not live near a major shopping centre where you have a good range of choice, you may be able to improvise an alternative or simply leave out whatever it is you cannot obtain, if it is not too important a feature of the design. We hope that the ideas throughout the book will inspire you to devise your own methods and ways of interpreting the themes.

BASIC MATERIALS AND EQUIPMENT
greaseproof paper or baking parchment
pencils
ruler
scissors
scalpel, with stock of disposable blades
multi-purpose adhesive
adhesive tape
cocktail sticks

MULTI-STAR SIGN CAKES

These two quite different designs are suitable for any birthday, representing the general zodiac theme, and they demonstrate how basic methods of cake decoration can produce the most spectacular results. In the Zodiac cake (left), the sun is surrounded by the symbols of all the signs of the zodiac, painted in gold on smooth white icing covering a simple round cake. This is a highly effective design that is very easily achieved. The Sun and Moon cake (right), with its sculpted sybols, may appear a much more ambitious project but this is based on quite simple techniques of moulding the shapes and painting them to enhance the details. The elastic texture of gelatin icing enables you to reproduce all the surface detail of objects used as moulds, in this case a plaster garden ornament and basic star-shaped kitchen mould (below). The method of using moulds allows great versatility in creating sculptured detail, as all sorts of shapes and textures can be achieved. Above, the sun and moon faces are shown with a decorative lion's head that is one of the icing moulds for the Leo birthday cake shown on page 34.

MULTI-STAR SIGN CAKES

As an introduction to our approach to the projects in this book, we present two beautiful cake designs that interpret the overall theme of the zodiac in their own distinctive and quite different ways. To begin with, this illustrates the idea that any single theme or subject can suggest a variety of possible decorations.

These cakes have been created using a number of the techniques that will be used throughout the individual star sign and theme cakes that follow. In this instance, rather than providing direct instructions on how to make the cake, we are explaining the concepts, ingredients and methods we applied with, where appropriate, suggestions as to how you could achieve similar effects by different techniques. This is to emphasize that you can feel free to adapt or reinterpret any of the designs. You need not be discouraged by feeling that you do not have all the necessary items to make the cakes exactly as they are shown, as it is often possible to find perfectly acceptable alternatives for various aspects of the decoration.

Our first design is a very simple and elegant iced cake bearing the images associated with each of the zodiac signs encircling a golden sun. This involves basic techniques of icing and painting the cake. Our second design is more ambitiously sculptural – the sun, moon and stars, moulded from gelatin icing, shine brilliantly above the richly painted cake. Artwork for the cake design to be found on page 126-127

Artwork for the cake design to be found on page 126-127

16

FOR THE ZODIAC CAKE
9in (23cm) round cake
2lb (900g) marzipan
1½lbs (675g) fondant icing
1lb (450g) gelatin icing
Food colour: gold
Ribbon

THE ZODIAC CAKE

This design is based on a 9in (23cm) round cake. We first marzipanned the cake in the usual way, applying the marzipan to a thin layer of sieved apricot jam spread over the cake. We then cut an additional sheet of marzipan about ½in (1.2cm) thick and trimmed it to a circle using the edge of a saucer as a guide. This was placed on top of the cake at the centre, fixed to the marzipan layer below with a little apricot jam. The cake was then completely covered with a layer of smooth white fondant icing.

Decorating the cake

The white discs displaying the zodiac symbols were made out of gelatin icing, cut into circles about 1-1½in (2.5-4cm) in diameter. For this, you could use a small circular biscuit cutter or cut around the edge of an egg-cup, or something else of suitable size. When the icing discs had dried, we transferred the designs onto them using graphite paper to trace down the symbols. Remember that if you use graphite paper, the discs should not be eaten. If you want the decoration to be completely edible, you can trace down the designs while the gelatin icing is still soft using the end of a cocktail stick to leave a faint impression. Finally, we painted over the traces using gold food colour and a fine paintbrush. To transfer the image of the sun to the large disc at the centre of the cake, we traced the design on greaseproof paper and used this as a pattern to impress the outlines of the sun on the soft fondant icing with a cocktail stick. To complete the design, all that remained was to paint the sun gold, following the outline impression and adding the linear detail.

FOR THE SUN AND MOON CAKE
Round cake, marzipanned and iced
4in (10cm) star-shaped mould
Plaster "sun face" garden ornament
Lengths of plastic rod
Lengths of inexpensive gold chain
Food colours: dark blue, ice blue, yellow, green, orange, red, gold, silver

THE SUN AND MOON CAKE

The basis of this design is a 9in (23cm) round cake, marzipanned and iced in the usual way. The decoration of the cake was simply painted on with food colours when the icing had dried. The three-dimensional symbols standing above the cake were all modelled out of gelatin icing simply by laying the icing over suitably shaped moulds, as described below. Although made of icing, these were intended to be removable parts of the decoration, not to be eaten. To obtain an unusual effect, almost as if the sun, moon and stars are suspended over the cake.

we fixed the symbols to colourless plastic rods that appear relatively unobtrusive but catch the light in attractive ways.

Painting the cake
The majority of the cake surface was stippled with dark blue food colour, leaving only the rainbow area over the curve at one side of the cake. In the rainbow, each band represents one of the four elements. The red and orange centre is overpainted with licks of gold to represent fire. The two shades of green lightening almost to yellow are symbolic of the earth and are overlaid with a pattern of broken, wavy lines in gold representing hills. The pale blue stands for water and the dark blue for air. We added tiny dots of gold here and there all over the dark blue surface to suggest stars in the night sky.

Moulding the symbols
We used two kinds of objects as moulds for the sun, moon and stars. The large gold stars were simply made by rolling gelatin icing out into a sheet and draping it over a star-shaped copper mould. This mould, which measures about 4in (10cm) across, was also used for the smaller stars. To make these, we trimmed the icing on the mould around the centre detail only; the small stars measure about 1in (2.5cm) across.

The sun and moon were both moulded over the same plaster ornament, bought from a local garden supplies store. To create the sun, we covered the whole ornament with gelatin icing. For the moon, we trimmed the icing to the centre of the mould to model only the face without the flame-like border.
You may be lucky in finding a similar ornament for use as a mould, but we can suggest two alternative methods of creating the sun and moon if you do not have a suitable object of this kind. These same methods can be used to make the stars, although you may find a star-shaped mould more easily as this is a readily available item of kitchen equipment.
The first method is to model the sun and moon faces out of marzipan or artists' modelling clay, the latter available in small packages from artists' suppliers. In either material, you can cut the basic outline shapes with a sharp knife and model the details of the face with your fingers, or even using a kitchen knife. Be careful not to create any undercut shapes that might trap the icing when you come to make the mould. The model should be a simple low relief of gentle curves. Allow the model to dry out completely before moulding the gelatin icing over the shapes.
The alternative method is to roll out

gelatin icing into a sheet and simply cut out flat shapes for each of the symbols. The iced decoration then obviously lacks the depth of the moulded symbols, but if attractively painted could look just as effective.

Painting the symbols
To colour the large stars, we began by painting each one with a different colour – one yellow, one red and one orange. When this colour had dried, we stippled over it with gold food colour, allowing the original colour to show through at the centre of each star but gradually working the stippling more densely to build up solid gold at the edges. The smaller stars we simply painted with silver food colour. The sun was first painted with deep red at the centre, blending out to orange around the flame-like collar. When these colours had dried, we used a pencil to sketch the facial details lightly onto the icing. (As with graphite paper, if you use a pencil it leaves graphite traces so the icing should not be eaten.) The face of the sun was then lightly stippled with gold, allowing the red to show through clearly defining the eyes, nose, mouth and dimples in cheeks and chin. We allowed the gold stippling to colour the edges of the face more densely, although still leaving some of the underlying colours showing through, then we used linear detail to emphasize the radiating pattern of the licks of flame around the face. For the moon, we began by drawing a curved line over the surface dividing the face roughly in half. To one side we applied blue food colour, to the other green. Using the same technique as for the sun, we stippled silver food colour over the blue side, leaving details of the eyes, nose and mouth showing through in blue, and creating a mottled blue and silver texture across that side of the face. On the green side, we built up the silver layer more solidly, so that the features appeared to be outlined in green on silver.

Assembling the decoration
The symbols were attached to sections of plastic rod varying in length, so that when the rods were stuck into the cake, the symbols formed a stepped arrangement. We fixed the symbols to the rods using very stiff royal icing, which forms a strong adhesive, but as the decoration is not intended to be eaten it could equally well be fixed with an ordinary all-purpose glue or even with adhesive tape. As a finishing touch we added varying lengths of gold chain, on which the smaller stars are suspended, to give movement and an additional shimmer to the design.

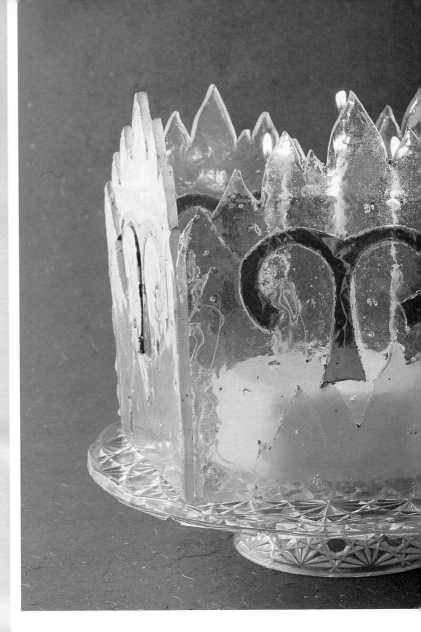

CHAPTER 2

ZODIAC CAKES

The signs of the zodiac provide great inspiration for cake decoration. Each sign offers a range of characteristics for the person born under its influence; a definite image, such as Taurus the Bull, Leo the Lion or Cancer the Crab; the physical elements associated with the sign – earth, air, fire and water; the special colours of each sign and individual objects such as the birthstones for each period of the zodiacal year. All of these items suggest visual interpretations that provide imaginative and innovative designs for birthday cakes and party treats – we have included many ideas for table decoration and accompanying dishes on zodiacal themes, as well as the spectacular and delicious cakes.

All the necessary instructions are included to enable you to produce the designs as shown, but we hope these pages will also give you plenty of inspiration to develop your own ideas and skills.

ARIAN FIRE

For the strong fire sign of Aries, cake decoration with a brilliant, active quality – stained-glass panels that emphasize the intensity of the candlelight. The technique of pouring sugar to create the panels is easily acquired, although you need plenty of time to create this design. As all the decoration stands outside the cake, you can choose the type of cake and icing according to taste.

Making the panels *To make the mould, roll out Plasticine into a sheet ¹/₄ in (6mm) thick.*

Put the sheet on a piece of aluminium foil and trace down your design.

Cut away the section of the mould to contain the first colour of sugar.

Paint the edges of the cut section with a little olive oil or corn oil.

Pour in the sugar, making sure it flows into all the edges of the mould.

FESTIVE CRACKERS

Crackers are simple to make but suggest many ideas for enhancing the visual excitement and festive spirit of your Arian birthday party. These examples incorporate an attractive wrapping paper printed with artistic impressions of heavenly bodies – entirely apt for a zodiacal celebration. You might prefer plain colours appropriate to the star sign, or bold patterning. You can give the crackers personalized name tags to identify place settings, with each cracker containing a tiny personal gift. When decorating the crackers, you can add to the glitter with Christmas tree baubles, metallic ribbons, brightly-coloured cellophane or foil papers. For a children's party, the measurements for the sections of the cracker (see over) can be scaled down to create lovely miniatures.

19

ARIES

21 March–20 April

Aries is, of course, a fire sign – its favourite colour is red, its metal is iron, its stone diamond. The Aries mixture of brilliant and combative characteristics is represented in a beautifully vivid cake decoration. The typical Arian is also known for being enterprising and adventurous and you may need to match those characteristics in acquiring new skills to produce this breathtaking centrepiece, but you will find that they are easily mastered. The main idea of the decoration is to create a stained-glass effect that allows the brilliance of the fire sign, represented by candles, to shine through. The interesting element is that the decoration is not on the cake, but surrounds it. It consists of panels of poured sugar, in the firelight colours of orange, yellow and red, featuring the astrological symbol for Aries. (The graphic symbols for all of the Zodiac signs are shown on page 61 and this design can be adapted for any sign.) Each panel is produced by pouring a hot sugar solution into a mould, working one colour at a time and allowing each colour to harden before the next is added.

FOR THE ARIES CAKE

cake (shape and size as required)
blocks of non-toxic modelling material (number as for required number of panels)
two ¼in (6mm) thick wood strips
metal foil
poured sugar (one batch per colour and one for fixing the panels)
food colours: yellow, orange, red
olive oil or corn oil

THE CAKE

Sugar quantity

The number of panels that you will need depends upon the size of your cake – you may get away with as few as three, or you can make as many as you wish. To determine the number, mark out the shape of your cake on a piece of greaseproof paper and draw a plan of the panels to surround it. To cut down on preparation time, you should make all the panels at the same time so that if, for example, you are pouring the orange-coloured sugar, you fill the appropriate sections of all the moulds with orange and then pass on to your next colour. The design as shown consists of six panels 8in (20cm) high, 6in (15cm) wide and ¼in (6mm) thick. The three main colours within each panel occupy roughly equal areas. One batch of sugar solution made up according to the recipe given (see page 73) was sufficient to fill one colour in all six panels.

Making the mould

For this, you need to buy blocks of a non-toxic modelling material such as Plasticine. It should be non-toxic in so far as it comes into contact with the poured sugar, which is an edible product, although we do not recommend that you eat the sugar panels, as they will do no favours to either your teeth or your waistline.

1 Begin by rolling the Plasticine into a sheet about ¼in (6mm) thick. To get a uniform thickness, use guiders in the form of two lengths of wood each ¼in (6mm) thick, which you will readily find at a DIY store or wood merchants. Lay the wood strips at either side of your Plasticine and roll it out until you find that the rolling pin is actually moving along the wood. This will give you the correct thickness. The size of the Plasticine sheet must be large enough to accommodate your whole design with a border to contain the sugar.
It can be difficult to roll out the Plasticine if it is cold. You can solve this by putting it in the oven at a very low setting to warm it through, when you will find it rolls quite easily. When you have finished, place the rolled-out sheet on a piece of aluminium foil.

2 Transfer the pattern for your panel onto a sheet of baking parchment or greaseproof paper and place this over the Plasticine sheet. Using a cocktail stick or the end of a paintbrush, trace along the lines of the pattern so they are scored lightly but clearly into the surface of the Plasticine.

3 Decide which sugar colour you will pour first, then use a sharp knife to cut out the appropriate section of the mould. Select a fine blade that enables you to cut accurately.
You should not cut through the aluminium foil beneath your mould. This may sound difficult, but in time you will learn to recognize whether you are touching the foil. If you do snag it, slip another sheet of foil underneath so that when you pour the sugar it hardens against the foil. If you let it set on the work surface, you will find it is virtually impossible to lift the panel free.

Pouring the sugar

The recipe for poured sugar is included with the instructions for making the Winter Cake on page 73.

1 When you have cut the first section of the mould, brush the cut edges lightly with olive oil or corn oil. This will enable you to lift out the next section of the mould cleanly after the sugar has hardened into the first section.

2 Make up the first colour of your sugar solution. Pour it into the mould in a slow, steady stream until the mould section is completely filled. Leave it for at least 20 minutes to allow it to harden before you proceed.

3 While the sugar is hardening, prepare for your next colour. Cut out the appropriate section of the mould and oil the edges, but do not apply oil to the existing sugar piece. You want the second colour to weld onto the first, so that the panel is self-supporting when it stands upright.

4 Continue building up the pattern in the same way until it is complete. When the panel is completely hard, remove the mould and trim away any pieces of Plasticine that adhere to the edges of the sugar. You will have no trouble stripping away the foil from the back of the panel. When you have completed the panels, they can be stored in the refrigerator until you wish to assemble them.

Assembling the panels

You will need another pair of hands to help you put the panels together. First, make up another pan of sugar solution to be used as an adhesive for the panels. Position the cake on its base and decide where to locate the surrounding panels. Hold one panel upright and, using a pastry brush, apply sugar solution liberally down one edge. Press the edge of the second panel against this adhesive side. You will find that they hold together quite quickly and you can proceed with the next panel. If in doubt, apply more sugar solution down the back of the join to strengthen it. If there are any unsightly blobs or dribbles, they will not be noticeable on the inside of the panels. Once you have assembled the stained-glass surround, all that remains is to place long tapering candles on the cake. Then light the candles and serve the cake to the admiration and applause of your guests.

Timing

This process, though simple, is time-consuming and you should make up the panels the day before the birthday celebration. Each batch of sugar can take as long as 15-20 minutes to produce, and each section of the stained-glass pattern requires at least 20 minutes to harden before you proceed. However, the most time-consuming part of the whole enterprise is scoring out the pattern onto the Plasticine sheet, cutting each section of the mould in turn and oiling the edges. When you add up all the various stages of the procedure, you will see that it does take a long time, particularly if you are making four or more panels. If you decide to be adventurous and use more colours in your design, this also lengthens the time you need for the whole project. We advise that you do not make the design too complicated the first time you try this. Be wary of including small pieces that need to be filled separately, or too many acute angles in a shape. Not only will you find it difficult to pour the sugar into a complicated mould, you may also find that pieces of the mould adhere to parts of the design and you will have a time-consuming and irritating job on your hands to scrape them off cleanly. We recommend that you don't embark on this project on a very warm or humid day, as sugar is sensitive to temperature changes and the surface becomes very tacky in hot or humid conditions.

FOR THE CRACKERS
thin cardboard
gift-wrap papers
cracker snaps
craft knife or sharp scissors
adhesive

MAKING CRACKERS

Aries has a warlike nature, so we thought crackers would be an amusing addition to the birthday celebration, evoking the noise and activity of combat.
Crackers are simple to make and you can choose from the wealth of beautiful paper designs to create crackers complementary to or contrasting with the themes and colours of your stained-glass design. You can use anything from coloured tissue to fancy gift-wrap paper, plain or printed. If you want each cracker to go off with a bang in the traditional way, you will need to buy the required number of cracker snaps to insert through the centres.
Personalized crackers carrying a nameplate for each guest make attractive "place cards" and with small gifts inside, something you have either bought or made yourself, they add to the party treats.

1 Cut a rectangle from thin cardboard measuring 5 × 6in (12 × 15cm). Roll it into a tube with the edges overlapped and fix them with adhesive.

2 Cut two more rectangles 6 × 8in (15 × 20cm) and form these into two longer tubes. These act as shapers.

3 Cut a piece of paper measuring 6½ × 14in (16 × 35cm). Place it right side down on your work surface and put the short cardboard tube at the centre, flanked by the two shaper tubes. Push a cracker snap down the centre of the tubes.

4 Draw a thin line of adhesive along the edge of the paper and roll up the cracker so that the edges overlap slightly and adhere. Slightly pull one of the shapers to make a gap between it and the tube at the centre of the cracker. Wrap a length of ribbon or twine around the paper at this gap and pull it to crimp the end of the cracker.

5 Drop a gift and motto into the open end of the cracker, then repeat the crimping process to seal the gift inside. Remove the shapers. We added decorated "collars" to our crackers. Inserted at each end, these also help to keep the cracker in shape.

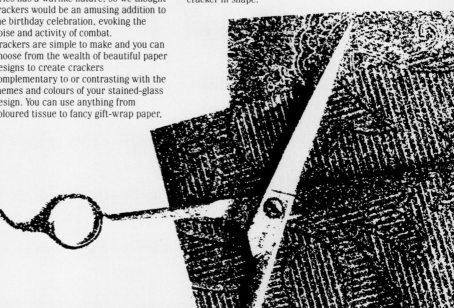

THE SIGN OF THE BULL

Inspired by the traditional inn sign, the design for Taurus presents the symbolic bull together with its constellation painted in vivid gold and red food colours. The sign is constructed to the appropriate size for the cake and simply placed over the iced cake when the moment comes for presentation to the birthday guest. Because the decoration is entirely self-contained, you can remove the sign before cutting the cake and keep it as a memento of the occasion. The sign is made from gelatin icing rolled out to a sheet of even thickness and modelled over a basic picture frame (above). Painting the bull is a straightforward process of applying the colours one by one when the icing has completely dried. The motif is uncomplicated but the lavish use of gold in the painting gives it a richly elaborate appearance.

Making the dough basket Model the basket over an upturned oven dish, cutting the base of the dish from rolled dough and forming the basketwork with strips woven around the sides.

Cut the ivy and vine leaf decorations from dough, varying the sizes, and assemble them on a baking tray. The decorative components of the design are arranged on the basket after baking.

DOUGH BASKET

The pale golden colour of the basket is the perfect complement to light cheeses and fruits, served as the final course of a dinner party or added to a buffet table for decorative effect. Although the baked dough strips are quite strong, the basket sides have an open-weave texture that may prove fragile. The contents should be piled on the basket base and allowed to rest only lightly against the sides.

TAURUS

21 April-21 May

Inspiration for the Taurus birthday cake was provided by the tradition of sign painting that has produced so many memorable images associated with the names of public houses and inns. Many of these depict animals or mythic beasts, so it seemed appropriate to conceive a strong image of Taurus the Bull in similar style. However, this approach could be equally applicable to any of the twelve signs of the zodiac.

The decoration for the cake, although edible in so far as it is made out of sugar, is intended to be completely separate from the cake itself so that you can remove it and keep it as a reminder of the special occasion. The sign is built over a picture frame. The size of the frame that you use may to some extent determine the dimensions of the cake, but if you have a particular size of cake in mind, you can have a frame made quite inexpensively to your own specifications. You can choose a simple or elaborate moulding for the frame, as the sign is made by covering the frame with gelatin icing, which is capable of picking up all the detail providing the texture of the icing is soft and pliable.

The second item that we have suggested for the Taurus birthday celebration comes into the category of edible containers (see also pages 98-101) and is adaptable to any style of entertaining. The attractively decorated dough basket makes an interesting and unusual feature for a buffet table or formal dinner party.

Artwork for the cake design to be found on page 126-127

FOR THE TAURUS CAKE

rectangular cake, marzipanned and iced
picture frame of dimensions to fit cake top
1-1½lb (450-675g) gelatin icing
food colours: cream, flesh pink, red, brown, black, gold

THE CAKE

Making the Taurus sign

The picture frame that we used measured 14 × 10 in (35 × 25 cm) and to cover this size you require 1-1½lb (450-675g) gelatin icing (see page 9).

1 Lay the picture frame on a completely flat surface or large cake board. Dust your work surface lightly with cornflour and roll out the gelatin icing into a sheet large enough to drape over the frame.

2 Lay the icing over the frame and, with hands lightly dusted with cornflour, smooth the icing into the detail of the picture frame and onto the flat work surface both inside and outside the frame.

3 Trim the excess icing close to the outer edge of the picture frame. Leave the centre intact, as this forms the canvas for your design. Allow the icing to dry overnight, or for at least 12 hours and preferably 24 hours.

4 To remove the frame from the icing sheet, turn the whole thing upside down and ease the frame out from the back. This is preferable to trying to pull the icing sheet off the frame from the front, as any uneven pressure at the sides might cause the icing to crack down the centre.

5 When you have released the frame, allow the icing sheet to dry for a further two hours so that the side that has been in contact with the work surface has time to dry out completely.

Painting the sign

We have chosen strong colours to paint the design, but you can adapt or change the scheme to colours of your own choice, perhaps following a colour theme for the party or using colours specially associated with Taurus.

1 Trace off the design onto a sheet of greaseproof paper and enlarge it to the correct size for your frame and cake. If you do not intend to eat the icing sign, you can trace down the design onto the gelatin icing using graphite paper to transfer the image. This is a simple method that leaves a clear outline, but you should only use it if the decoration will not be eaten. If you intend to eat the iced sign with the cake, trace the lines of the design with a cocktail stick to leave a faint impression in the surface of the icing while still soft.

2 Using gold food colour and a brush, outline the shape and detail of the bull and the pattern of the constellation, and paint the lettering in gold. At the same time, work on the details of the frame that appear in gold. (You can alternatively use

a gold marker pen for this work, again only if the decoration is not to be eaten.) The gold colouring repels other colours, so if you apply this first, subsequent colour applications will not spoil the detail if you happen to work over the gold lines.

3 Use cream food colour diluted to a pale tone to paint the shape of the bull, working inside the gold outlines. Allow the colour to dry.

4 Apply additional detail to the bull by stippling with flesh-toned food colour to create shadow on the stomach, back, legs and horns, and under the garland around the neck.

5 Mix red and brown food colours in a ratio of 2:1 to create the brick red colour for the background. The best effect is achieved by using strong food paste colours and not diluting them too much with water. Paint the background all over with brick red, then stipple lightly over it while the colour is still wet to give a textured finish. Using the same colour, fill in the details of the flower garland already outlined in gold. Then add the linear detail of the nose, eyes, ears and horns.

6 To complete the design, paint the black-lined area of the picture frame. Allow this to dry for several hours, as black food colour tends to remain tacky for longer than other colours. When the painted sign is completely dry, simply place it on top of the iced cake.

Timing
To make sure that the icing sign is completely dry, you must leave it for up to 24 hours after modelling it over the picture frame. Make sure that you also allow sufficient time for painting the design and waiting for the colours to dry between applications where necessary.

——DOUGH BASKET——

This delightful dough basket, decorated with ivy leaves and vines and baked to a pale golden colour, is quite simple to make using the recipe for hot-water crust pastry on this page. The only equipment that you need is an ovenproof container as a mould for the basket. We used the bottom half of a chicken brick, but any suitable oven dish will do. The dish has to be quite thoroughly greased before you start work and we recommend that you don't attempt this work in a very hot kitchen, otherwise the surface of the container becomes too slippery for the dough pieces to adhere properly.

1 Place the oven dish upside down on the work surface and cover the outer walls and base with a layer of white vegetable shortening. This forms a slightly adhesive layer on which you can arrange the dough pieces, and later prevents the dough from sticking to the sides of the container when the basket is baked.

2 Roll out the dough and cut a piece large enough to cover the base of the dish. Then cut a number of strips of dough about 1/2in (1.2cm) wide and long enough to hang down over the sides of the dish from the covered base.

3 Position the dough strips at about 1in (2.5cm) intervals around the sides of the dish. Use a little egg wash to fix the end of each dough strip to the dough base previously applied. The vegetable shortening on the sides of the dish should help to keep the strips in position.

4 Cut two long strips of dough about 1/2in (1.2cm) in thickness. Start to weave one of these strips around the side of the dish at a point about halfway down the side, passing alternately over and under the short vertical strips. Use the second strip to complete the weaving all the way around the dish. Press the ends of the strips together where they join on either side of the dish, securing them with a little egg wash.

You may need someone to help you with this stage, as if the dough strips are quite long, they can begin to slip down the sides of the dish before you have completed the weaving process. To help secure them, use a little egg wash to fix them to the short vertical strips.

5 Cut another long strip of dough, twist it and arrange it around the rim of the upturned dish. Allow it to rest on the work surface and press it against the vertical strips forming the sides of the basket. This twisted strip will form the top edge of the basket.

6 Roll out the remaining dough to a thickness of about 1/4in (6mm). Cut out ivy leaves and vine leaves in a range of sizes. Arrange some of the leaves to lie flat on a baking sheet. To create curled leaves, such as those decorating the top of the basket, drape them over the curves of a small oven dish so that they will bake in curling shapes.

7 Cut some very long, thin strips of dough and arrange them on the baking sheet in curling patterns to form vine tendrils. Roll some of the remaining dough into balls the shape and size of

grapes and place these on the baking sheet.

8 For a golden finish, brush all the dough pieces with egg wash before putting them into the oven. Bake at 375°F (190°C)/gas mark 5 for 50 minutes to one hour, checking that the pastry does not become too brown. After baking, allow the basket and decoration to cool before assembling the pieces.

Decorating the basket
The vegetable shortening should make it easy to release the dough basket from the dish after baking. If any part has stuck, simply ease it away from the dish with a knife.

Turn the basket right way up and arrange the leaves, tendrils and grapes around the sides and rim. If you want the basket to be completely edible, use an edible paste, such as a flour and water mixture, to stick on the decoration. Alternatively, if you do not intend to eat the basket, you can use a multi-purpose adhesive and make sure that it dries completely before putting any food into the basket.

HOT-WATER CRUST PASTRY

1lb (500g)/2 cups plain flour
1 tsp (5ml) salt
1 egg yolk
4oz (125g)/1/2 cup butter
4oz (125g)/1/2 cup lard
6 fl oz (175ml)/3/4 cup water

Sift the flour and salt into a warmed mixing bowl. Make a well in the centre and add the egg yolk. Cover the egg yolk with the flour.
Heat the butter, lard and water in a saucepan and bring to the boil. Make sure that the fat melts before boiling point is reached. When the mixture is boiling, pour it onto the flour and egg, and mix vigorously with a knife.
When the mixture cools slightly, turn it out onto a lightly floured surface and knead until the dough is smooth. Cover the dough in plastic film and leave it to rest in a warm place for 25-30 minutes, then use it immediately.

25

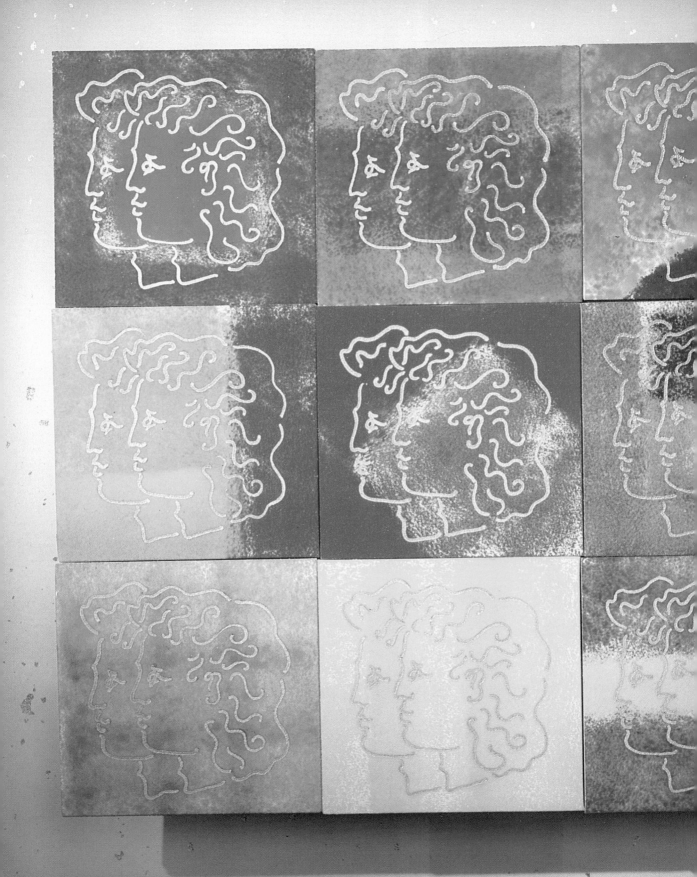

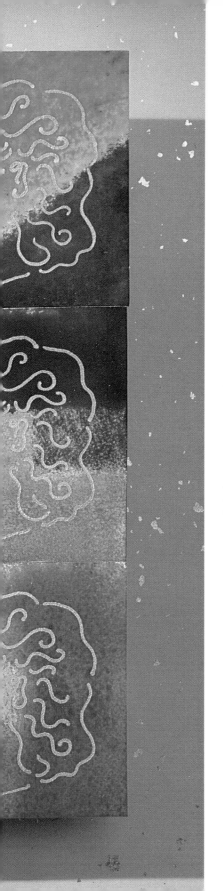

GEMINI – THE TWINS

An artist-inspired motif depicting the twin heads of Gemini is used in two different ways to form the decoration for a birthday cake. The brilliantly coloured background (far left) consists of painted squares of gelatin icing with the motif outlined in silver. On this rests the cake (left) sculpted into the twin-head motif and outlined in silver on pure white. The coloured squares can alternatively be used to decorate the top of a square cake.

PARTY DISGUISE

The quicksilver character of Gemini, changing from day to day, is represented in a stunning party mask sparkling with diamante chips. The various elements build the disguise layer upon layer, using bright colour and glittering highlights to emphasize the dual nature of this excitingly active birth sign. Other themes and ideas that can be used for decorating basic mask shapes are included in the Masquerade section on pages 106-109.

27

GEMINI

22 May-21 June

Among many and varied traits, the Gemini character is known for being up-to-date and very versatile as well as adaptable. The classic image is of duality, often represented as two profiles face to face with each other. As the basic idea for our cake decoration we have chosen the aspects of adaptability and versatility, together with the Geminian love of colour and, reflecting the duality of the sign, we have produced a design that can be interpreted in two ways.

The main image for the cake decoration is a twin-head motif depicted as a repeat pattern on a multi-coloured background. The drawing of the male twins is based on the imagery of artist and writer Jean Cocteau. The background colour is inspired by the repeat silkscreen prints of Andy Warhol, such as his famous images of Marilyn Monroe, and it is applied using a small sponge roller, an item associated with silkscreen printing that should be available from your local art supplies store. The roller enables you to create variations of texture within the colour blocks. The multi-coloured design can be used either as the covering for a square iced cake, or as the background to the second interpretation of our motif, a cake carved to the shape of the twin heads and iced in white and silver.

Geminis are known for their ability to argue a point very forcefully on one day, and on the next day to take a completely opposite stance argued with equal conviction. In effect, you can never be quite certain which face the Gemini person is going to present to the world, or what lies behind the image that you see. The party mask that we have created in a brilliant combination of red, black and silver strikingly represents this element.

Artwork for the cake design to be found on page 126-127

FOR THE MULTI-COLOURED SQUARES

1lb (450g) gelatin icing
12in (30-cm) square cake board
food paste colours: red, yellow, orange, blue, green, pink, purple, silver
sponge roller

The multi-coloured design

The coloured squares are created out of gelatin icing (see page 8), although the finished decoration is not necessarily to be eaten with the cake. It consists of nine individual 4in (10 cm) squares, for which you need 1lb (450g) gelatin icing. If you intend to use this as the background to the carved cake, you need a 12in (30cm) square cake board on which to assemble the icing squares.

1 Dust your work surface lightly with cornflour and roll out the gelatin icing as thinly as possible. Cut nine 4in (10cm) squares and allow them to dry for several hours.

2 Copy the design on paper to a size that will fit within the 4in (10cm) square. If you do not intend to eat the icing, the design can be transferred to the squares using graphite paper. If you do intend to eat it and do not want graphite traces, draw the design on greaseproof paper or baking parchment and use a cocktail stick to trace the outlines on each square while the icing is still soft.

3 Using food paste colours, mix up all the colours you need in individual saucers. Do not add too much water - the colours should be strong and vibrant. Load one colour onto the sponge roller and apply it as required. You may wish to make each square a different colour, or extend colours from one square into another. You can also vary the textures according to the way you manipulate the roller. Work with one colour at a time until all the squares are painted.

4 Following the traced lines underneath the colour, outline the twin motifs using silver food colour. When the squares are complete and dry, assemble them on the cake board, fixing each square in place with a dab of royal icing.

If you are using the coloured squares to decorate a square cake, simply ice the cake and position the coloured squares in sequence on the top.

8in (20cm) square cake
1lb (450g) marzipan
sieved apricot jam
1lb (450g) fondant icing
food colour: silver

THE GEMINI CAKE

To create the cake sculpted in the form of the twin heads, you need to bake an 8in (20cm) square cake and enlarge the artwork for the design to fit that size. You require enough marzipan to cover the cake and 1lb (450g) fondant icing.
The finished cake is intended to be positioned on top of the coloured squares already assembled on a cake board. To make sure that the cake does not stick to the underlying icing squares, which you may wish to save, we suggest that you place the cake on a very thin board while applying the marzipan and icing, then trim the board to the lower edges of the cake. This will form a clean base that will do no harm to the coloured icing squares when the cake is put in place.

1 Lay the artwork on top of the cake and using a sharp knife, trim the cake to the edges of your pattern.

2 Spread the top of the cake with sieved apricot jam. Roll out the marzipan to a thickness of about $1/4$ (6mm). Use a sharp knife to cut the outline of the twin heads in the marzipan sheet. Position the marzipan piece on top of the cake.

3 Roll out the remaining marzipan. Measure the depth of the cake and cut a strip of marzipan to that depth and long enough to wrap around the sides of the cake. Use sieved apricot jam to fix the marzipan strip to the cake.

4 Dust the work surface lightly with cornflour. Roll out the fondant icing into a sheet large enough to drape over the top and sides of the cake. With fingers dusted lightly with cornflour, smooth the icing to the surface of the cake and around the edge. Use a sharp knife to trim away the excess icing, then leave the icing to dry for about one hour.

5 Place the paper pattern on the top of the cake and trace the design using a cocktail stick to impress the lines lightly in the icing. Remove the pattern and paint the lines on the icing with a fine paintbrush and silver food colour.

PARTY MASK

Since Gemini is a sign well known for its changeability, this mask is designed to add layer upon layer of disguise. The mask itself is bi-coloured to represent the duality of Gemini, one side being dark and sombre and the other vivid and flamboyant. The face is covered with a mesh veil, another partial concealment. Over this, we have mounted twin smaller masks, also divided down the centre to reiterate the theme.
The basis of the design is a white full-face mask which you should be able to obtain quite easily from any store selling party or carnival novelties. You also require two smaller mask sizes.
To begin with, divide the mask roughly down the centre and paint one side red and the other black. You can use an inexpensive poster paint or gouache for this. Then spray the edges of the mask lightly with silver paint. The two smaller masks are each coloured singly, one red, one black, then sprayed with silver. Create the glittering line down the centre of the large mask by sticking on small pieces of flat-backed diamanté, using a quick-drying adhesive. Stretch the red mesh over the mask and secure it at the back with adhesive. Fix some diamanté pieces to the mesh. Then put the smaller masks in position and highlight them with diamanté, again using quick-drying adhesive to secure the components. As a finishing touch, we have added a fiery red feather.
The mask is intended to be carried in front of the face, so you need a piece of dowelling about 12in (30cm) long and $1/4$in (6mm) thick. Wrap this in fine red cord of the type readily available from haberdashery counters. Keep the cord in place at top and bottom by tying it with thread or sticking it to the wood. Fix the dowelling just inside the chin of the mask, using a strong cement adhesive.
If you prefer, instead of mounting the mask on dowelling you can pierce the sides of the mask and thread through ribbon ties, so that the mask can be worn directly on the face.

29

SWEET PASTRY SHELLS

An exotic fruit dessert presented in scallop shells made from sweet pastry is a deligthtful variation on the shellfish theme appropriate to a Cancerian birthday. You can obtain real scallop shells from your local fishmonger to use as moulds for the pastry (above). The individual sweet pastry shells are filled with a layer of rich crème patissière before being decorated with colourful fruit slices (right). To give additional lustre to the fruits, they are coated with a clear apricot glaze, which can be flavoured with a liqueur of your choice for added piquancy. Individual servings can be decorated with two or three mint leaves for a fresh effect (below right), with each place setting surrounded by small delicacies and decorations continuing the seashell theme. Alternatively, you might prefer to serve up all the shells together on a large plate flooded with delicious fruit purees that can be swirled into a pattern of mingling tastes and colours.

CANCER
THE CRAB

A crab modelled from marzipan and lavishly decorated with colours and metallic lustre climbs over a cake base consisting of a simple round madeira sponge carved to a gentle slope. Royal icing covering the marzipanned cake forms a smooth base for the colour work. While the blended colours used in this example add impact to the image, the crab can look equally splendid if painted in one single, strong colour on a differently coloured ground, so beginners in cake decoration need not feel this design is beyond their skills. The basic processes of carving and modelling the cake are very straightforward.

Modelling and painting the cake
The crab is an impressive creature, but the picture above shows how easily it is created by cutting out the required shapes from marzipan sheets. The cut edges of the marzipan are rounded down to complete the curving, shell-like effect.

When painting the crab, you need to mix up all the colours that you wish to use so that they can be applied in rapid succession to each section of the crab and blended together while still wet. Take care not to make the colours too liquid, or they will run down over the curves.

31

CANCER

22 June-23 July

The Cancerian birthday cake takes the splendid form of a large crab emerging from the sea. Although the finished product looks quite awe-inspiring, it is remarkably simple to achieve with basic techniques of carving and modelling. The cake is lightly carved to form a sloping platform on which the shape of the crab is modelled with layers of marzipan. The colours are applied to a covering of fondant icing. We have chosen colours not necessarily associated with the sign of Cancer, but the rich blues and purples echo the watery theme. The painting technique allows the wet colours to merge and form complex gradations of hue and tone. However, if you are not confident of reproducing this effect, the cake could look just as stunning with the crab painted in a single colour, such as a vivid red.

For each of the zodiac signs there are a number of associations and it is amusing and often surprising to see how you can develop the theme throughout the preparation and decoration of party foods. For the water sign of Cancer we have created sweet pastry shells, moulded from scallop shells, as containers for individual servings of a sumptuous fruit dessert.

Artwork for the cake design to be found on page 126-127

FOR THE CRAB CAKE

9in (23cm) round madeira sponge
2lb (900g) marzipan
sieved apricot jam
1½lb (675g) fondant icing
food colours: light blue, dark blue, purple, golden yellow, brown
edible silver lustre powder

THE CAKE

Modelling the crab cake

The design is based on a 9in (23cm) madeira sponge. You need enough marzipan to cover the cake and provide the shapes for the crab, and 1-1½lb (450-675g) fondant icing as the final layer.

1 Start carving from a point about 2in (5cm) from one edge of the cake and make a sloping cut towards the opposite side, leaving a thickness of about 1½in (4cm) from the base on that side.

2 Gently round off the corners and edges of the cut areas so that the overall shape is soft and curving.

3 Cover the cake with sieved apricot jam and apply a layer of marzipan over the whole surface.

4 Draw the shapes of the crab body, legs and claws on greaseproof paper and use this as a pattern for cutting the shapes from marzipan. For the main body, roll out the marzipan to about ½in (1.2cm) thickness. For the upper body, use a thinner layer about ¼in (6cm) thick. Put the two body pieces together.

5 Cut the shapes of the legs and claws from marzipan, varying the thicknesses so that the claws at the front of the cake are thicker and more imposing than the legs trailing behind the crab. Round off the edges of all the cut shapes.

6 When you have cut all the marzipan pieces, begin assembling them on the cake. Position them carefully on the sloping surface to give the effect of the crab emerging from the sea. Use sieved apricot jam to secure the pieces. Allow the completed cake to stand for two or three hours before icing.

7 Dust your work surface with a little cornflour and roll out the fondant icing into a sheet large enough to drape over the whole cake. Lay the icing over the cake and, with fingers lightly dusted with cornflour, smooth the icing into the modelled detail. Trim off the excess and allow the icing to dry for several hours, or possibly overnight.

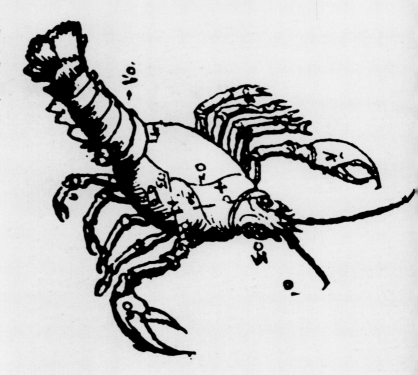

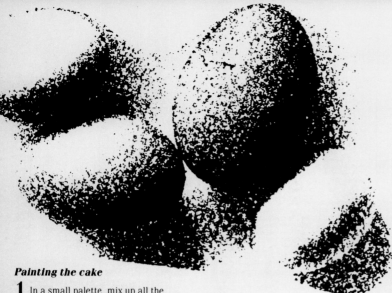

CRÈME PÂTISSIÈRE

6 egg yolks
4oz (125g)/¹/₂ cup caster sugar
1¹/₂oz (50g)/4¹/₂ tbsp flour
³/₄pt (450ml)/2 cups milk
pinch of salt
vanilla pod

Beat egg yolks and sugar until thick and light. Stir in the flour. Scald the milk by bringing it just to the boil with the salt. Add the vanilla pod to the hot milk. Leave to infuse for 10 minutes.
Remove vanilla pod and reheat milk to boiling point. Whisk boiling milk into egg mixture, return to pan and whisk over gentle heat until boiling. Make sure the crème is smooth before letting it boil — if lumps form as it thickens, remove from heat and beat until smooth. Cook crème gently for 2 minutes until flour is completely cooked. Remove from heat and allow to cool.

Painting the cake

1 In a small palette, mix up all the colours you require for painting the crab so that you can apply them rapidly and blend the colours together. Don't make the colours too wet, or they will run down from the raised sections onto other parts of the cake.

2 Paint one section at a time, applying bands of colour and fading the edges of one colour into another. In our example, you will see that the colours pass from dark blue through a brighter blue to purple, then back to a dark blue-purple.

3 Paint the top and sides of the cake surrounding the crab with golden yellow to represent sand, then stipple on a little brown food colour to create texture.

4 When you are satisfied with the colour effects, allow the paint to dry, then dust the body of the crab with edible silver lustre powder to give it a luxurious sheen. We also added non-edible pieces of diamanté to catch the light and enhance the presentation, but if you do this, you must ensure that the pieces are not eaten.

Alternative methods

The design for the crab cake as it is presented here depends on careful painting technique. If you are not confident about painting directly onto the modelled cake, you can alternatively create the crab out of pre-coloured gelatin icing or marzipan. Then all you need to do is cut out the required shapes and place them on the cake.

Timing

This cake can be decorated in two separate stages: first shaping and covering the cake; then painting it. The icing needs to dry out for several hours, or overnight, before you begin painting.

FOR THE SHELL DESSERT

scallop shells, one per person
sweet pastry
selection of fruits
crème pâtissière
apricot glaze

—SWEET PASTRY SHELLS—

To make the sweet pastry shells, you need to acquire scallop shells from your fishmonger to use as moulds, or you can use ceramic shells of the type intended for serving fish starters, providing they are heatproof.

1 Rub the back of the shell moulds lightly with butter or margarine. Roll out the sweet pastry very thinly and cover each shell with pastry on the outside.

2 Press the pastry gently into the detail of each shell and trim the edges by pressing your fingers lightly against the edge of the shell. It is important that the pastry cannot curl underneath the shell during baking, or it may break when you try to remove it.

3 Place the shells on a baking tray and bake at 300°F (150°C)/gas mark 3 for about 20 minutes, or until the pastry shells are a pale golden colour. Leave to cool for about five minutes, then gently ease the pastry off the shell mould.

4 Fill the shells by piping crème pâtissière into the centre, then apply slices of fruit over and around the crème pâtissière and finish with apricot glaze.

SWEET PASTRY

4oz (125g)/³/₄ cup flour
pinch of salt
1¹/₂oz (40g)/4¹/₂tsp caster sugar
2 egg yolks
¹/₂tsp (2¹/₂ml) vanilla essence
2oz (60g)/¹/₄ cup butter

Sift the flour into a bowl and add the salt and caster sugar. Cut the butter into cubes and work it into the flour with the fingertips. Add the egg yolks and mix with a fork. Gather the mixture together and to mix thoroughly, work it in batches by pressing over the work surface with the heel of the hand. Press the dough into a ball and wrap in plastic film or aluminium foil. Chill for 30 minutes or until firm.

APRICOT GLAZE

8oz (250g) apricot jam
3 tbsp (45ml) hot water or liqueur

Sieve the apricot jam and stir in the water or liqueur.

THE CLASSICAL LEO

The lion, the noble king of beasts, calls up many associations going back through centuries of history and mythology. This design returns to classical times, taking its themes and motifs from the great empires of Greece and Rome. Classical statuary and architecture are assembled on a baseboard decorated with jewel-like Greek patterns. The lion's head, an apparently elaborate sculpture, is simply created by moulding gelatin icing over a small garden ornament (left). The decorative columns at the back of the design are also moulded from sections of sculpted cornicing. The cake itself is contained within the fallen column, given fluted detail by marzipan layers which in turn are covered with fondant icing painted with a delicately marbled texture.

Modelling the lion *Cut the flame shapes from a marzipan sheet using a paper pattern.*

Model the face and nose in thicker marzipan layers to develop the relief effect.

When the modelling is complete, lay a sheet of fondant icing over the cake.

Paint the detail of the flames and the lion's face on the dried fondant icing.

LION IN FLAMES

The majestic head of a lion emerging from tongues of flame is an appropriately strong symbol for this vigorous fire sign. Like the classical design, it has a dramatic quality that will greatly appeal to the theatrical Leo. Although the cake appears very detailed and elaborate, the modelling of the lion's head is quite simple to achieve, by building up layers of marzipan graded in thickness to develop the relief effect of the emerging head. Given a smooth, clean finish with a covering of fondant icing, the head can then be painted with simple blocks of colour or complex textures imitating reality, as in this example. Merged and blended colours give a flickering life to the flames and the face of the lion is painted with careful attention to detail, shading the tones to enhance the modelling of the form and using drybrush textures to create the effect of the lion's fur.

LEO

24 July-23 August

For the design of the Leo birthday cake we have looked back to the myths associated with the sign, and in particular to the classical connections. The ancient civilizations of Greece and Rome are represented in architectural ruins, statuary, and classic Greek patterns. The noble lion's head, appropriately finished in gold, is modelled in gelatin icing using a small garden ornament as the mould. You may find something similar at a garden centre, or you may come across another kind of ornament portraying a lion that could be used as a pattern for the icing version. However, if you do not have something suitable, this does not mean that you cannot attempt the cake design. If you look at our second presentation for a Leo cake, you will see the lion's head emerging from tongues of flame that is modelled out of layers of marzipan. You could easily adapt this idea for use in the first design, creating the lion's head out of marzipan and covering it with fondant icing to achieve a detailed, uniform finish. Artwork for the cake design to be found on page 126-127

FOR THE CLASSICAL LEO CAKE

10in (25cm) square cake
14in (35cm) square cake board
2-2¼lb (900g-1kg) marzipan
sieved apricot jam
4lb (1.85kg) gelatin icing
1¼lb (565g) fondant icing
food colours: blue, orange, grape violet, gold

THE CLASSICAL LEO

In the design as shown, it is the fallen column behind the lion's head that is made of cake. The other elements are modelled in icing and you can proceed stage by stage through the design creating the pieces one by one. If you wish to include a greater amount of cake, we have suggested below an alternative way of constructing the circular columns. The design is on a grand scale, reflecting the Leo's love of the dramatic and the innate creativity of this sign. The baseboard for the cake and decorations is 16in (40cm) square.

Covering the baseboard

The baseboard is covered with a sheet of gelatin icing on which the Greek patterns are painted with food colour. For this you require about 2lb (900g) gelatin icing.

1 On a work surface lightly dusted with cornflour, roll out the gelatin icing into a sheet large enough to cover the cake board. Lay the icing over the board and trim it to the edges. Allow it to dry for about two hours before proceeding.

2 Draw up the pattern of the Greek design on greaseproof paper, enlarging it as necessary. Transfer the design onto the icing using graphite paper (this icing is not intended to be eaten).

3 Paint the details of the pattern using the food colours of your choice and a fine paintbrush. Allow the colours to dry.

4 Mix sky blue food colour to a fairly watery consistency. Cover the painted section of the board with a sheet of cardboard or thick paper to mask it off while the blue is applied to the remainder of the icing sheet. Use an airbrush or mist-sprayer to apply the colour, either as a flat or gradated tone. Allow it to dry.

5 To create the impression of shadows on the surface, spray areas of the board very lightly, at random, with grape violet colour mixed to a watery consistency. You can again mask off the areas that are to remain unshadowed.

If you are not confident of painting the whole board, you can alternatively colour the gelatin icing with blue colouring before you roll it out, then lay the blue sheet over the board. To add the Greek pattern, roll out a separate sheet of white icing and position it across the blue, angled from one corner as shown in the photograph. Then trace down and paint the Greek design as above.

Making the cake column

For the fallen column, we used a 10in (25cm) square cake cut in half to produce a rectangle 10 × 5 × 5in (25 × 12.5 × 12.5cm).

1 Gently carve off the edges of the cake along its length to produce a more rounded, columnar shape. Carve the ends irregularly to appear as broken column ends. Cover the cake with a fine layer of sieved apricot jam.

2 Roll out 1-1¼lb (450-565g) marzipan into a sheet large enough to cover the entire cake. Lay the marzipan over the cake and smooth it down. Don't worry if it creases at top and bottom as this will add to the effect of the fractured column.

3 Roll out 1lb (450g) marzipan and cut strips 1in (2.5cm) wide and the length of the column. Wrap one piece around each end of the column, then lay strips lengthwise on the cake at 1in (2.5cm) intervals to create the effect of fluting around the column. Fix the strips in place with a little apricot jam. Trim and round off the edges where the lengthwise strips meet those circling the column. (It is possible to cut the fluted shapes from one piece of marzipan, but it can be difficult to wrap this around the cake without it stretching out of shape.) Allow the marzipan to dry for four to six hours.

4 On a work surface lightly dusted with cornflour, roll out 1¼lb (565g) fondant icing into a sheet large enough to cover the whole cake. Lay the icing over the cake and, with fingers lightly dusted with cornflour, gently smooth the icing into all the detail, picking out the fluted edgings and pressing the icing to the top and bottom of the column. Trim any excess icing and allow the cake to dry for four or five hours.

5 Paint the icing with a marbled pattern using grape violet to create the shading and gold to trace the veins in the marble. You can sponge or spray on the grape violet to obtain a delicate effect, but paint the veins crisply with a fine brush. (For further detail on marbling, see the Libra birthday cake on page 42.) Allow the colours to dry and position the cake on the baseboard.

An alternative method of creating the marbled effect is to work some colour into the icing before you apply it to the cake. Begin by applying a dab of grape violet colouring to the fondant icing and knead the icing to work the colour through partially. After 15-20 seconds, add a dab of dark blue and continue working for another 10-15 seconds. When you roll out the icing sheet, you should find that it has taken on a swirling pattern of colour reminiscent of the texture of marble.

Moulding the lion's head

Assuming that you have a suitable ornament to use as the mould for the lion's head, all you need do is take 1lb (450g) gelatin icing and, while it is still soft and a little warm, roll out the icing into a sheet and drape it over the lion's head, pressing it into the detail. Trim the edges of the icing and allow it to dry before removing it from the mould. Paint the finished head with gold food colouring.

Alternatively, you can model the lion's head from marzipan layers, as explained in the instructions for the second Leo cake. Place the head on a thin cake board. Apply fondant icing over the marzipan and trim the excess. Then, carefully cut the board to the edges of the modelled head. When the icing has dried, you have a solid, firm head that can be positioned on your baseboard.

Creating the decorative columns

Like the lion's head, the two remaining decorative pieces that complete this design were made from gelatin icing moulded over a solid pattern, in this case, pieces of ornamental cornicing obtained from a DIY store. Simply roll out the icing and drape it over the moulds, pressing it into the pattern detail. Allow it to dry before removing it from the moulds. Use grape violet colouring, applied with an airbrush, mist-sprayer or sponge, to add shadow detail to the finished columns. When all the icing pieces are complete, assemble the full design on the baseboard.

Alternative method

If you wish to include more cake in the design, you can alternatively make the rounded columns from 6in (15cm) round cakes stacked to form a column and carved into irregular and decorative shapes. You can add marzipan fluting in the same way as for the fallen column and cover the whole cake with fondant icing. You would require about 1½lb (675g) fondant icing to cover one column made from three or four stacked 6in (15cm) cakes.

FOR THE LION IN FLAMES CAKE

10in (25cm) round cake
4lb (1.85g) marzipan
sieved apricot jam
2lb (900g) fondant icing
food colours: yellow, orange, red, brown, purple

——LION IN FLAMES——

This striking design for the fire sign of Leo is easily modelled by building up layers of marzipan on top of the cake. Successive layers are made progressively thicker to develop the head in strong relief on the cake top. The sculpted head is then covered with fondant icing on which the colouring is painted. Our design is based on two 10in (25cm) round cakes sandwiched together with a filling layer, but you can use any type of round cake to your own taste. To cover the cake and create the lion's head you need about 4lb (1.85kg) marzipan and to ice, 2lb (900g) fondant icing.

Modelling the lion

1 Cover the cake with a thin layer of sieved apricot jam. Roll out 12oz (350g) marzipan and use the tin in which the cake was baked to cut a 10in (25cm) diameter circle. Place the circle of marzipan on top of the cake. Cut a long strip of marzipan to the depth of the cake and long enough to wrap around it. Apply marzipan to the side of the cake and allow it to dry for about two hours.

2 Trace the design on greaseproof paper, enlarging it as necessary. Roll out 12oz (350g) marzipan and cut out the outer sections of the design, following the paper pattern. Position these on top of the cake, fixing them with a little apricot jam.

3 Roll out another 8oz (350g) marzipan, making a slightly thicker sheet than before. Cut the middle section of the design and position it on the cake, fixing it with apricot jam. Roll out another 12oz (350g) marzipan, again to a thicker sheet than the one before. Cut out the lion's

face and position it on top of the cake.

4 For the lion's nose, roll 8oz (200g) marzipan into a ball and flatten the base on your work surface. Using a rolling pin, slope the ball from the highest point, which should be about 1½in (4cm) above the work surface. Smooth the sides to form the bridge of the nose. Using the paper pattern, cut the outline of the nose and position the marzipan piece on top of the cake. Gently round down the edges to blend it to the rest of the lion's face.

5 On a work surface lightly dusted with cornflour, roll out 2lb (900g) fondant icing into a sheet large enough to cover the whole cake. Drape the icing sheet over the cake and trim it to the cake sides. Gently smooth it into the detail on the top of the cake. Allow the icing to dry for eight hours or overnight.

Painting the cake

To create a very detailed effect, we have painted the flames with blended colours and have developed quite a lot of texture in the lion's face. If you prefer, you can paint the various sections of the design with solid colour, which gives a very vivid, strong effect.

1 Make up the required shades of red, yellow and orange food colours. Paint the flames, first applying the red, then brushing in the orange and yellow. Merge the colours while still wet. Paint some of the flames with solid colour.

2 Paint the detail of the lion's face in brown, using drybrush technique to develop the furry texture. To do this, dip the brush in the colour, then splay the bristles and drag them across the icing. Follow the picture of the finished cake as a guide to the texture and shading of the lion's face.

3 Outline the edges of the flames with gold. Fill in the background around the outer flames and the jewel pattern within the design with dark purple. When all the paint is dry, dust the cake lightly with edible gold lustre powder. As the final touch, wrap gold ribbon around the cake.

CAMEO CAKE

As befits the Virgo subject, the classical cameo presents a wealth of beautiful detail. The apparently elaborate design is surprisingly easy to achieve using straightforward icing techniques, but it can be tailored to the time and effort that you wish to put in, since some of the detail that has been described here with piped icing can be simply painted on the surface if preferred. In this presentation, the plain oval of the cameo is surrounded by a decorative wreath of ivy leaves made from gelatin icing, dusted with gold lustre to heighten the rich detail. Alternatively, the cameo can be cleanly presented in a plain gold frame, as shown opposite.

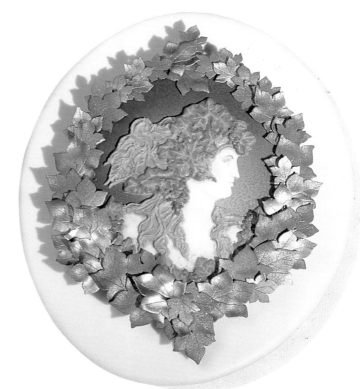

DECORATIVE CRACKERS

Crackers are not just for Christmas celebrations. These examples show how, by careful selection of decorative wrapping papers and colourful ribbons, you can create a delightful range of party crackers suitable for any time of year.

Pipe the outline of the design.

Flood the outline with pale royal icing.

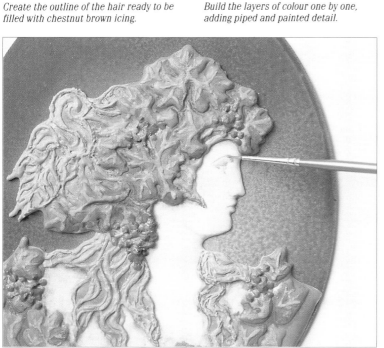

Create the outline of the hair ready to be filled with chestnut brown icing.

Build the layers of colour one by one, adding piped and painted detail.

CREATING THE CAMEO

The basic oval shape is cut from a sheet of gelatin icing and the background is sprayed with gradated colour. The outline of the cameo is then piped and flooded in with flesh-tinted royal icing. Subsequent layers, for the hair and dress, are created in the same way, with piped or brushed detail laid in over the solid colour areas and the facial features finely painted. To create an icing frame for the cameo (below), simply mould gelatin icing over a correctly sized frame, trim the edges cleanly and apply gold food colour.

VIRGO

24 August-23 September

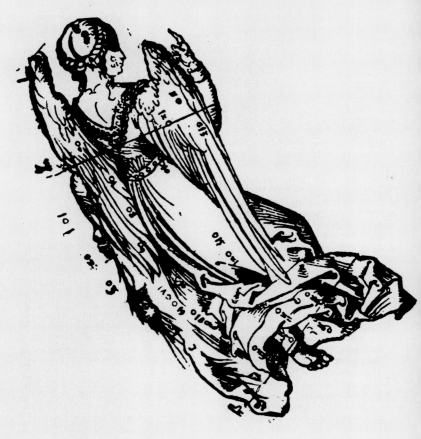

Virgo has been cast as the daughter of Jupiter and as the Goddess of Justice and was frequently symbolized as a young girl renowned for her purity. The characteristics associated with this birth sign include creativity and attention to detail. These we have represented in a decorative interpretation of the classic cameo that has a richly elaborate appearance but is actually quite simple to achieve. The subtle colouring of the cameo reflects the fact that Virgo is an earth sign.

All the decoration is created on a removable plaque of gelatin icing that sits on top of an oval cake. This enables you to save the cameo as a memento of the occasion — having gone to great lengths to create such a magnificent item, it would seem inappropriate to eat it. The sculptured effect of the cameo is created by piping the outlines using an icing bag, then flooding more icing into the outlined shape. If you are inexperienced in this technique, don't be put off. A few minutes practice with the icing bag before you begin work on the final design will give you plenty of confidence.

For an additionally festive touch, we have pictured pretty crackers made from colourful wrapping papers and decorated with ribbon bows. Under the Aries birthday section on pages 18-21 you will see some alternative ways of decorating crackers together with the basic instructions for making them. Artwork for the cake design to be found on page 126-127

FOR THE VIRGO CAKE:

8in (20cm) oval cake
1lb (450g) marzipan
1lb (450g) fondant icing
1/2lb (225g) gelatin icing
royal icing made with one egg white
food colours: flesh, brown, green, violet
icing bag and no. 2 nozzle

THE CAKE

Creating the cameo

Our demonstration is based on an 8in (20cm) oval cake, and we used the cake tin as the guideline for cutting the oval piece of gelatin icing on which the cameo is painted. For this size, you will need about 1/2lb (225g) gelatin icing.

To obtain a smoothly gradated background for the Virgo portrait, we used an airbrush to apply the colour. This is a specialized and relatively expensive piece of equipment, but you can get a similar effect using a clean, new toothbrush. Dip the toothbrush lightly in the food colour, then pull your finger back along the tips of the bristles to spray colour onto the icing piece. (If you prefer, you can create a plain single-coloured background by colouring the icing before you roll it out.)

1 Roll out the gelatin icing into a smooth sheet and cut the oval plaque. Colour the background with an airbrush or toothbrush, working first with brown, then with green to build up the graduated shades.

2 Draw the design in outline on tracing paper and transfer it to heavy cardboard. Cut out the silhoutte with sharp scissors.

3 Place the cardboard pattern on the icing and use a needle to draw around the edge, scratching the outline into the surface of the icing.

4 Make up a batch of royal icing, using one egg white, according to the recipe on page 8. Split the icing into two bowls and mix one with a little flesh-tint food colour to make a very soft flesh tone. Then add a little more egg white to the icing to give it a slightly thinner consistency. When you lift the spatula out of the bowl and allow the icing to fall back in, it should leave a trace for a few seconds before finding its level again.

5 Fit a no. 2 nozzle to a small icing bag. Beginning at one extreme edge of the cameo pattern, pipe lightly along the outline of the design. Do not worry if you lose some detail in the curls and waves of the hairline, but try to get the profile clean and accurate.

6 With the outline complete, take a teaspoon and pour some of the flesh-coloured icing into the area inside the outline. This will spread and find its own level, but will be contained by the piped outline. If the icing does not spread into all the detail, use a small paintbrush to ease it into the angles and curves. When this is complete, allow the icing to dry. It may need as long as 12 hours.

7 Draw the shape of the hair on greaseproof paper or baking parchment. Lay this on the icing and prick out the outline with a pin (the pinpricks will be covered by the next line of piping).

8 Add some brown food colouring to the remaining flesh-coloured royal icing. Use a piping bag fitted with a no. 2 nozzle to pipe around the hairline in the same way that you originally outlined the whole design.

9 Fill the outlined shape with the coloured icing as in the previous stage, easing it into all the detail of the design.

10 Take your second bowl of royal icing and colour it green. Outline the top of the dress with the icing bag, then flood colour into the shape with a teaspoon as before.

Developing the detail
You now have the basis of the cameo iced on two levels. As you can see from the photographs, we have gone on to make a third level of icing forming the ivy leaf and flower details over the hair and dress by piping and flooding the shapes in the same way as before. However, if you feel the piping has become too intricate by this stage, you can paint the remaining detail using a slightly thicker consistency of royal icing. You can see the effect of this in the cameo where we have painted the strands and curls of the hair over the basic layer of brown icing.

1 To test the consistency of the green icing, load a paintbrush with the icing and try painting a few strokes on your

work surface to see if the icing holds its shape. If not, add a little icing sugar and try again.

2 When you have the correct consistency, paint the ivy leaf shapes forming a crown over the hair and a wreath around the neck of the dress. If you paint these on one level, try to create undulating, natural leaf forms. If you prefer, you can wait for the first painted layer to dry and add details of the leaf veins to enhance the decorative effect.

3 To create the small bunches of fruits, add grape violet food colour to the remainder of the flesh-tinted royal icing and use a paintbrush to apply small dots of colour, gradually modelling them into the clusters of grapes on the headdress and neckline decoration.

4 Using the brown royal icing, thickened slightly if necessary, paint individual strands and curls of hair swirling over the basic icing layer.

5 To complete the cameo, paint the delicate features and shadows on the profile using food colour and a fine paintbrush. Draw simple lines and shapes with the tip of the brush and just smudge

the shadows gently to blend them to the flesh tint.

Timing
Although it may seem that the first flooded layer of royal icing is quite thin, in fact there is some depth to it and you are advised to allow it to dry for as long as 12 hours or overnight before you begin the next level. If you are too eager to add more work before the icing layer is ready to receive it, you will find small crush lines and splits occurring that will spoil the overall effect.
This applies to each level of icing – you should wait until it dries completely before adding more. Depending on the technique you use to develop the detail of the design, you will certainly need to spread your work on the cameo over two days, perhaps longer.

Framing the cameo
We have suggested two ways of presenting the cameo. One is an ivy wreath, adding to the classical theme, created from leaves made of gelatin icing. Cut the leaf shapes from a rolled out sheet of gelatin icing. Allow some to dry flat but arrange others perhaps over a rolling pin or supported on a cotton wool base, to create irregular, natural-looking curves. When they are dry, paint the leaves in tones of deep green. You will need quite a number of leaves, graded in size and colour, to form a generous wreath.
The second presentation shows the cameo within a gold frame, which is also made from gelatin icing. You need to find a frame that will fit the design and mould a sheet of icing over it, picking up all the detail. Then, you simply trim the excess on the inside and outside edges of the frame and allow the icing to dry completely.
When the icing frame has dried, colour it with gold food colour and a touch of red, to give an antique, distressed look, then fit it to the cameo.

Decorating the cake
Our 8in (20cm) oval cake was marzipanned and iced with fondant icing in the usual way. Allow the icing on the cake to dry out for several hours before you apply the plaque. Since the intention is that the plaque should be removable, it is essential that neither the cake nor the cameo retains surface moisture that will allow them to stick together. As a precaution, you can cut an oval of baking parchment and slip it between the cameo and the cake, then be sure that you remember to remove it before the cake is cut.

41

THE LIBRAN SCALES

The design for the romantic, discerning Libran demonstrates that beautiful flowers are equal to a fortune in gold when weighed in the balance of the Libran scales. The cakes forming the base of the scales are decorated with delicate marbling painted over fondant icing. The weighing pans are easily moulded from gelatin icing, using ordinary saucers as the moulds, and the rest of the design is quickly constructed using a length of wooden lath and pieces of cardboard, all painted silver. The overall effect not only represents the idealistic approach to life typical of Libra, but also appeals to the Libran love of exquisite objects.

Decorating the cake Cut two rectangles of cake to create sloping sides, then cover them with marzipan and fondant icing.

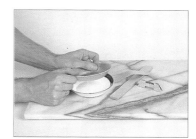

To make the weighing pans, roll out gelatin icing, press it into a saucer mould and release the icing when it has dried.

Position the painted wood on top of the cake, add the details of the weighing mechanism and set the pans in place.

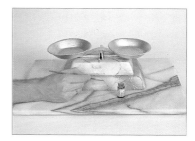

If you wish, you can finally retouch the painted details of the marble veining to enhance the effect.

Decorative accessories
All Librans respond to beautiful objects and will appreciate the care you take to produce personalized decorations for the birthday setting. The Libran love of refinement is exemplified in a formal invitation card and envelope made from elegantly marbled papers (left) that is the perfect complement to the painted finish of the Libran scales cake.
Create an atmospheric mood with romantic lighting and the special beauty of fresh flowers, combined in a simple hanging decoration for an attractive wall light (right).

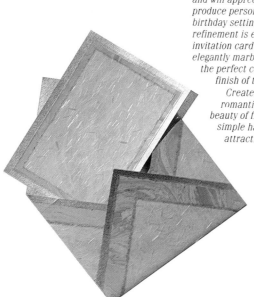

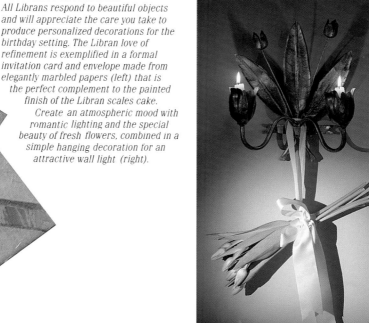

LIBRA

24 September-23 October

Romantic, idealistic, creative, appreciative of art and natural beauty – all of these terms describe the Libran personality. The cake that we have designed for the Libran birthday illustrates the romantic idealism characteristic of this sign. The Libran scales demonstrate that the beauty of flowers is worth much more than their weight in gold. Our image is a long way from the classic association with the scales of Justice, but it is typical of the way the heart may rule the head in the judgement of a true Libran. The scales themselves, in which the cake forms the base, are a beautiful combination of delicate marbling and shining silver, appealing to Libra's artistic taste and appreciation of the finest quality in all things. Our pictures also show ideas for additional decorations that contribute special personal touches to the party mood.

FOR THE LIBRA CAKE

10in (25cm) square cake
1½lb (675g) marzipan
sieved apricot jam
1-1½lb (450-675g) fondant icing
food colours: pink, red, silver
8oz (225g) gelatin icing
12 × 1in (30 × 2.5cm) wood strip
cardboard strips
chocolate bars covered with gold foil
fresh flowerheads

THE CAKE

Covering the cake

The base of the cake is formed from a 10in (25cm) square cake cut into one rectangle 10 x 6in (25 x 15cm) and one 7 x 4in (17 x 10cm). These are lightly carved to create sloping edges. They are covered with marzipan and fondant icing (see pages 8-9) over which the marbling is applied.

1 On each rectangle of cake, mark a line all around the top ½-¾in (1-2cm) from the edge. Holding a sharp knife angled from the line towards the base of the cake, cut sloping edges on each side of the rectangle.

2 Cover each cake with a thin layer of sieved apricot jam. Roll out about 1½lb (675g) marzipan and use this to cover the top and sides of each piece of cake.

3 Take 1-1½lb (450-675g) fondant icing and, on a work surface lightly dusted with cornflour, roll it out to form icing sheets large enough to cover each of the cakes. Drape the icing over the cake and smooth it down on all sides.

4 On the larger cake that forms the bottom tier of the scales, apply a light, even colouring of delicate pink, applying the food colour with an airbrush, mist-sprayer or sponge. Keep it very light and allow the white icing to show through the colour in some areas. Allow the colour to dry for a few minutes before adding the marbling detail.

5 With a fine paintbrush, use a darker shade of pink to create a fine tracery of lines roughly following the pattern of pink and white areas on the cake. To create additional highlights, add a second series of light "veins" painted with silver food colour.

6 Colour the smaller cake in the same way but more lightly, creating faint blushes of pink on the white background and marking out the vein pattern in silver only. When the marbled effect is complete, place the small cake on top of the larger one, positioned at the centre.

Constructing the scales

Various materials are required to construct the additional detail of the scales. The weighing pans are modelled from gelatin icing. These are balanced on a wooden support, with pieces of cardboard forming the additional elements of the weighing mechanism. All of these components are painted silver. We recommend that you do not try to make the entire structure from cardboard, as the pans have some weight and need the firm support of the wood strip placed across the top of the cake. The piece of wood needs to be 12in (30cm) long and 1in (2.5cm) wide.

1 Roll out 8oz (225g) gelatin icing. Cut two circles large enough to fit inside two small saucers. Press the icing circles into the saucers and trim the edges. Allow the icing to dry completely before removing each piece from its mould and painting it silver.

2 Cut a rectangle of cardboard about 3 × 1in (8 × 2.5cm). Fold it in half along

the length and stand it on the work surface to form an inverted V-shape. Cut a strip of cardboard to the same width and length as the wood strip. Paint the wood and the cardboard pieces silver and allow them to dry.

3 Place the length of wood across the top of the cake. Position the V-shaped piece of card crosswise over the wood strip, at the centre of the cake. Over this, place the strip of cardboard aligned with the wood. Balance the weighing pans at either end of the wood so that they hold down the ends of the cardboard strip.

Finishing touches
When the cake is completely assembled with the scales in place, load one of the weighing pans with small bars of chocolate, wrapped in gold foil to represent gold bars. In the other pan, place a selection of beautiful flowerheads. Our scales contain romantic red roses and pink tulips, complementing the colours of the cake and the theme of the decoration.

—FLOWER DECORATIONS—

Fresh flowers are the perfect decoration for the Libran birthday, especially those flowers that have a refined, classical beauty. Our hanging bunch of tulips bound with fine ribbon is a delightfully simple but elegant way to display these well-shaped blooms, but there are dozens of equally effective ways of decorating with flowers.

Flower petals strewn down the table between shining cutlery and glasses add a rich carpet of texture and perfume to the party setting. Alternatively, dishes of damask rose petals make beautiful and unusual candle holders – place a single, graceful candle in each dish with a handful of petals at the base. The flickering candlelight adds an extra dimension as well as releasing some of the fragrance of the flower petals. Pot-pourri could be added to the petals for an extra touch of colour, but beware of using too much as the smell can be quite overpowering.

Another effective idea for hanging decorations is to obtain small ball-shaped pieces of florists' foam. Studded with fresh or dried flowers and trailing ivy, these could be hung on the chair backs as markers for the place settings, with a pretty name card attached, and might also make individual gifts that your guests could take with them from the party. You could turn these into delicious "pomander" balls by adding spices such as star anise and whole cloves. Alternatively, for a bit of fun, you could

stick pale golden popcorn and attractive pasta shapes to the foam ball, then add a few small flowerheads and leaves to give freshness and colour.

A beautiful summer straw hat can be garlanded around the crown with a rich wreath of flowers and then hung on the wall as a decoration. In all instances, flowers are particularly well displayed near to a light source, to bring out the texture and colour of the petals and leaves. Natural candlelight is the perfect complement.

You can make a trailing decoration to hang along a mantleshelf or bannister rail by putting together tiny wired posies of flowers, herbs and ribbons and tying these into a long string or cord. A garland of this kind can also make a lovely table centre, wound between candlesticks or dishes of fruit. Don't neglect herbs in your flower decorations, not only for their fragrance but because they are also very beautiful to look at.

You can display flowers in an unusual container that itself makes a wonderful contribution to the finished effect. Shells are especially lovely flower containers, whether the large conch shells with their soft pink interiors, stunning pure white clam shells brimming with a simple mass of flowerheads, or even small shells found on your holiday at the beach, each containing a small posy to mark a place setting.

—FORMAL INVITATION—

A Libran will appreciate a prettily presented, formal invitation to the party. Our design uses layers of beautiful marbled papers, matching the elegance of the Libran cake, with an emphasis on the pale pinks and mauves that are favourite Libran colours. For both the card and the envelope, the papers are stuck together in overlapping layers to create the decorative border effects. Spray adhesive is the cleanest and most efficient type of adhesive to use for this.

For the envelope, we cut a large square of silver paper to which we stuck a smaller square of Italian pink marbled paper. Over this, we added a yet smaller square of thin, textured white paper that allowed some of the pink to show through from underneath. The envelope is simply made by folding in the corners of the square as shown and sticking them down on three sides, leaving one flap open for insertion of the card.

The card is made from the same three layers of paper as the envelope, stuck to a plain white card on which you can write your message on the reverse. The card is planned to the correct dimensions for it to slide easily inside the envelope.

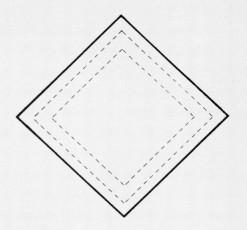
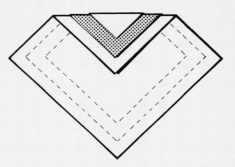
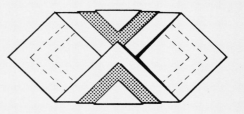
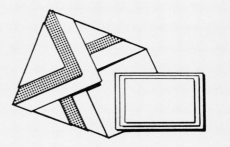

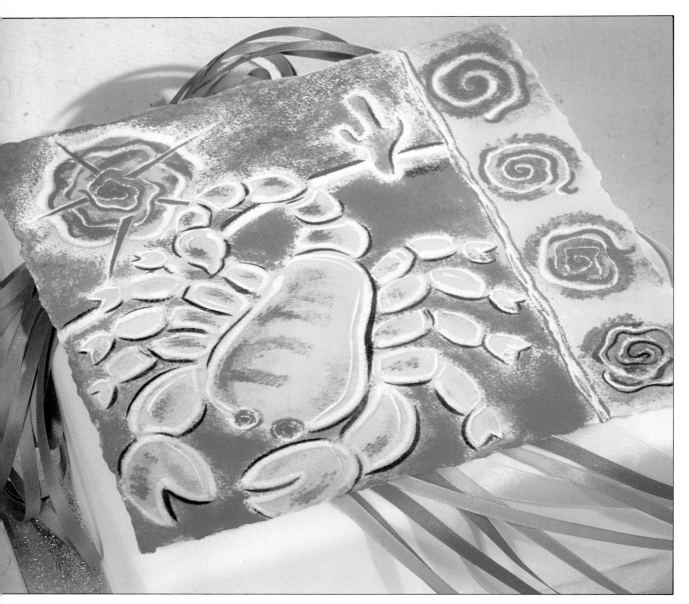

THE SCORPION

The striking symbol of Scorpio is
represented with bold colours and shapes
inspired by the rich expressionism of
Latin American art. The design is painted
on a plaque of gelatin icing that is
simply placed over the top of a
square cake (left)

and decorated with brilliantly coloured
ribbons. Alternatively, you can apply the
colour work directly to the top of a
fondant-iced cake. The surface of the
gelatin icing is textured and incised
before colouring to give an added
dimension to the piece. The painting
techniques are very free and vigorous, so
you do not need to be a practised artist to
produce an excellent result. In fact, the
design is well-suited to the uninhibited
character of children's painting, so even
quite young children can join in the fun of
creating the cake decoration.

CARVING AND PAINTING TOOLS

The outline of the design for the scorpion decoration (opposite) is incised in the icing before the colour is applied. The best tools for this technique are lino-cutters with V- or U-shaped gouges. For applying the base colour, we used a sponge roller, as shown here, an applicator generally sold by artists' suppliers for use in silkscreen printing.

SCORPIO FOOTBALL HELMET

The Scorpio person is a bold and determined character, with perhaps a touch more aggression than many of the other zodiac signs. A symbol of the armour of a modern-day champion, this football helmet is easily created with minimal skills of cake-carving and colour application. The basic form of the cake is shown in the pictures below, together with the simple method of shaping the visor, which is constructed from lengths of thick cord, strengthened with wire pushed through the centre. The end result will be a particular delight to young Scorpios with ambitions to emulate their sporting heroes.

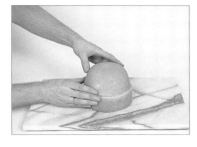

Shaping the helmet *Make one round cake and one cake baked in an ovenproof bowl and put them together as shown.*

Using a sharp knife, round off the top of the bowl-shaped cake and cut a recess into the front of the helmet.

Constructing the visor *Cut lengths of thick cord reinforced with wire and bind them together with strong thread.*

47

SCORPIO

24 October-22 November

Powerful, determined and energetic are words that aptly describe the Scorpio character. We have interpreted this in two entirely different but equally appropriate designs for cakes for the Scorpio birthday. The first, based on the symbol of the scorpion, takes as the design theme the brilliant colours and bold shapes typical of Latin American wall hangings and paintings. The plaque of gelatin icing is textured and carved before colouring. To obtain the loose, vibrant mood of the image, the colour is applied with various types of sponges or can even be finger-painted. Children can have a wonderful time helping with the painting of this cake, choosing whatever method of colour application suits their interests and capabilities.

The nature of Scorpio also includes an aggressive tendency and great perseverance. These qualities suggested to us that Scorpios would have been well suited to the life of the knights of old, going into combat as courtly champions. However, our modern champion is to be found on the football field, carrying his helmet and body armour like his medieval ancestor. The second cake represents this image as a visored football helmet decorated in bright colours, with the scorpion image prominently displayed.

Artwork for the cake design to be found on page 126-127

FOR THE SCORPION CAKE
10in (25cm) square cake, marzipanned and iced
12oz (350g) gelatin icing
piece of needlepoint canvas
lino-cutting tools
food colours: yellow, orange, red, blue, green

THE SCORPION

The following instructions explain how to make a plaque of gelatin icing carrying the design, with the idea that this is not eaten with the cake but is removed before cutting, and can if you wish be saved as a memento of the birthday. It is also possible to work directly on the cake top using fondant icing. There are certain differences in the approach if you are using fondant icing meant to be eaten, and these are separately described

below, following the step-by-step instructions for the gelatin icing plaque. The cake shown is 10in (25cm) square, and to make the plaque for the top you will need about 12oz (350g) gelatin icing. An unusual item that you need to give texture to the icing is a piece of needlepoint canvas with an open-weave texture. The design is carved into the icing, and for this the ideal instruments are simple lino-cutting tools, available from artists' suppliers. Alternatively, you can use a potato peeler with a V- or U-shaped gouge tip. Use a new tool, so that the end is sharp. Before you begin, enlarge the scorpion design on this page to the size that you require and trace it onto a sheet of paper.

1 Roll out the gelatin icing into a thick sheet large enough to accommodate a 10in (25cm) square. To create texture in the icing, roll it on ordinary flour, not cornflour as would normally be used. The coarseness of the flour gives a vellum texture to the gelatin surface.

2 Press the piece of needlepoint canvas into the surface of the icing. Position it in different ways on the surface, changing the direction to create an impressed cross-hatched texture. Trim the icing to 10in (25cm) square, leaving the edges slightly uneven, and roll the edges with the end of a paintbrush to thin them out. Leave the icing to dry for about 15 minutes, but no more. The next step is to carve the icing and it needs to be firm but not completely dry.

3 Trace off the design onto the icing sheet using graphite paper to transfer the image (the icing must not be eaten if you use the graphite trace).

4 Using a lino-tool or potato peeler, start to carve the lines of the design in the icing. Place the cutter at the end of the line and push it cleanly through the surface, to take out a shallow channel of icing. The purpose of this is to create incised lines that will remain white when you apply colour to the raised areas remaining between them. You can carve every line or, alternatively, just enough to give the scorpion shape and definition.

5 When the carving is complete, mix the food colours that you need in separate saucers. They should not be too watery, but should be fluid enough to create differences of light and shade. Begin by applying the lightest colour, the golden yellow, using a sponge roller to spread it quickly over the surface. It need not be completely even, as the texture of the paint adds to the overall impression.

6 Use a small piece of sponge to paint orange over the yellow. Highlight the body of the scorpion and dab the colour into the suns bordering the design. Continue in the same way, using sponges or your fingers to add detail in red, blue and green. To sharpen the image finally, paint some linear detail using a fine paintbrush and dark blue food colour. Allow the colours to dry for several hours.

7 Mount the gelatin plaque on the marzipanned and iced cake. Raise it slightly from the surface by sitting the plaque on a square of marzipan about 1/2in (1.2cm) thick. To complete the effect as shown, swathe opposite corners of the cake with ribbons of varying widths and colours complementary to the design. Remove the plaque before cutting the cake.

Using fondant icing
If you wish to apply the scorpion design

directly to the top of a fondant-iced cake, make the icing layer about 1/4in (6mm) thick to allow for the incised detail and allow it to dry for about 12 hours before you start the carving and colour work. As you will be eating the icing with the cake, do not use graphite paper to trace down the design. Draw your pattern on greaseproof paper or baking parchment and transfer it down on the fondant icing by impressing the lines lightly through the paper with a cocktail stick. Then follow the carving and colouring processes as above.

FOR THE FOOTBALL HELMET CAKE

6in (15cm) round cake
6in (15cm) bowl-shaped cake
sieved apricot jam
1-1¼lb (450-565g) marzipan
1-1¼lb (450-565g) fondant icing
food colours: red, yellow, black, silver
thick red cord
thin wire

——SCORPIO FOOTBALL—— HELMET

To make the basic shape of the helmet you need one 6in (15cm) round cake and one cake baked in an overproof bowl that measures 6in (15cm) in diameter across the rim. So that the cake will slide easily out of the bowl after baking, prepare the bowl by coating the sides with butter or margarine, then add 1-2 tablespoons of flour and tap the bowl to spread a dusting of flour all over the greased layer. Tip away the excess flour before putting in the cake mix.
For marzipanning and icing the cake, you need 1-1¼lb (450-565g) marzipan and the same amount of fondant icing. Before you begin shaping the cake, look at the pictures on page 47 which demonstrate the underlying form of the helmet.
For the grille-like visor, you require thick red cord and some fine wire that can be run inside the cord to give it the strength to hold its shape when bent into place. The wire should be very thin, but flexible and strong.

1 Turn the bowl-shaped cake upside down and put it on top of the round cake. The bowl-shaped cake now has a slightly flattened top corresponding to the base of the bowl in which it was baked. If you want to make the helmet as a perfect hemisphere, lightly carve the top of the cake to round off the edges.

2 To create the area of the helmet

where the footballer's face would be visible, use a sharp knife to mark the front of the cake with a shape like a rectangle with slightly rounded corners. Cut into the cake along this line to a depth of about 3/4in (2cm) and take out the oblong section. Trim the edges and recessed surface of the carved section as cleanly as possible.

3 Cover the entire surface of the carved cake with a fine layer of sieved apricot jam. Roll out the marzipan on a work surface lightly dusted with cornflour. Drape the marzipan sheet over the cake and gently smooth it to shape, pressing it into the recessed front of the helmet. It will readily stretch cleanly over the curves, but if you do get creases in the marzipan try to concentrate them at the back of the cake where they will be less noticeable. Trim the edges of the marzipan to the base of the cake.

4 Cover the cake with fondant icing following exactly the same process as that for applying the marzipan, but before you begin, just moisten the recessed section of the helmet with clean water. This encourages the icing to stick to the marzipan, reproducing the carved detail accurately. Allow the cake to stand for several hours until the icing has firmed up slightly.

5 Trace the scorpion motif on greaseproof paper or baking parchment. Position it on the top of the helmet and go over the lines with a cocktail stick or skewer to impress them lightly in the icing. Colour the scorpion red with a background of yellow, either in flat colour areas or with some shaded detail as shown. Paint lines of red and silver bordering the shape around the motif.

6 To create the red stripe over the back of the helmet you can simply paint a broad band of red food colour or, if you are not confident of painting, you can colour some fondant icing with red food paste colour and cut a strip of icing to be laid over the curve of the helmet. The ear pieces can be painted or added as icing cut-outs in the same way.

7 Make the visor from several lengths of red cord reinforced with wire pushed through the centre. To prevent the cut ends of cord from unravelling, bind them with strong sewing thread. Shape each piece for the visor by bending the strengthened cord to shape, then bind the pieces together with thread. Fit the finished visor to the helmet and bend it into position so that it hugs the sides of the cake.

49

THE ARCHER

For the Sagittarian, an elegant design incorporating the symbols of the Archer, horseshoe prints on the top of the cake and a quiverfull of slender arrows. The horseshoe shapes are cut from a layer of marzipan (right) that is placed over the original marzipan layer sealing the cake, creating the hoofprint impressions. The finishing touch is a golden wreath of bay leaves.

50

Making the arrows
The arrows consist of pieces of slender wood dowelling topped with delicate flight feathers and tipped with fine points cut from pieces of cardboard. The flights and tips are individually glued to each length of dowelling (right).

PARTY DESSERTS
For the sophisticated Sagittarian, or anyone with a sweet tooth who appreciates beautifully presented food, we have created additional party desserts that taste as good as they look – key lime pie (above left), Pavlova (above) and poached pears (left). Care in the presentation adds to the party theme. The pear has been poached to a deep purple colour (a Sagittarian favourite) and is served among swirls of delicious fruit purée of orange (apricot) and yellow (pineapple) representing the fact that Sagittarius is a fire sign.

SAGITTARIUS

23 November-21 December

The image of Sagittarius the Archer is represented in this design by horseshoe prints apparently impressed in the surface of the cake and a quiver of slender arrows. The striking blue colouring of the iced decoration is offset by clear red and shining gold decoration. Making the cake requires simple skills of marzipanning, icing and painting. The arrows are intended to be kept as a memento of the occasion and are made of completely inedible materials; the flights and tips are cut from cardboard. The laurel wreath, also an inedible feature, consists of bay leaves sprayed with gold.

FOR THE SAGITTARIAN CAKE

9in (23cm) round cake
2lb (900g) marzipan
sieved apricot jam
1-1½lb (450-675g) fondant icing
food colours: berry blue, ice blue, red, grape violet, silver, gold
edible silver lustre powder
thin wood dowelling or barbecue skewers
cardboard pieces
gold foil stars
scarlet ribbon
40 bay leaves (fresh or dried)

THE CAKE

Decorating the cake

The design is based on a 9in (23cm) round cake. The marzipan covering, which is applied in two layers to create the shapes of the horseshoes, requires 2lb (900g) marzipan, and you will need 1-1½lb (450-675g) fondant icing.

1 Cover the cake with a layer of sieved apricot jam. Roll out the marzipan and apply it to the top and sides of the cake in the usual way.

2 Roll out the remaining marzipan to a sheet at least ¼in (6mm) thick. Cut it to

a circle to fit the top of the cake. Within the circle, cut out the shapes of two horseshoes. Spread the top of the cake with a little apricot jam and position the second marzipan layer. Allow the cake to stand for several hours before icing.

3 Roll out the fondant icing on a work surface lightly dusted with cornflour, making a sheet large enough to drape over the top and sides of the cake. Brush the marzipanned cake with a little boiled water (or brandy or sherry to taste) to moisten the surface and create a tacky surface to which the icing can adhere.

4 Lift the icing sheet on the rolling pin and drape it over the cake. With hands lightly dusted with cornflour, smooth the icing to the surface, gently pressing it into the horseshoe details. Trim the excess icing at the base of the cake. Leave the iced cake for several hours before applying the colour.

5 Using a thick artist's brush, stipple the whole surface of the cake with a dark shade of berry blue food colour. The stippling technique enables you to achieve a deep shade of blue that also retains its brightness. It is not important to achieve a uniform tone. Some areas may be slightly darker and more mottled than others, which increases the effect of a darkening sky. Build up the colour more densely inside the horsehoes to give emphasis to the shapes.

Making the quiver

The quiver is made from marizpan and coloured when the shape is complete. For this, you need ¾-1lb (350-450g) white marzipan.

1 Roll out the marzipan to a thickness of at least ½-¾in (1.2-2cm) and cut a rectangle 9 × 2in (23 × 5cm). Cut one end of the rectangle into a semicircle.

2 Gather up the remaining marzipan and roll it out into a sheet about ¼in (6mm) thick. Cut four strips ¼in (6mm) wide and about 3in (8cm) long. Arrange these to form bands around the top and centre of the quiver as in the photograph. Cut two circles of marzipan about ½in (1.2cm) diameter and position these on the quiver as shown.

3 Paint strips of bright red between the raised bands on the quiver. Colour the rest of the quiver with grape violet. When the colour has dried, dust silver lustre powder along the edges, Finish by attaching a length of gold cord to top and bottom and arrange it to form a gentle curve as shown.

Making the arrows

For these you require very slender lengths of wood dowelling, about 1/16in (2mm) thick, or you can use slim wooden skewers as available for kebabs and barbecue cooking.

For the flights and tips of the arrows you require thin cardboard, which may be the colour you require or can be painted with an appropriate colour. To make the faceted effect of the flights and tips, you require four cardboard pieces for each. The arrows that are inserted in the quiver can be made half-length, with only the flight-end completed.

1 Cut the dowelling into three 12in (30cm) lengths and three 6in (15cm) lengths and paint the pieces red.

2 Cut the shapes of the flights and tips from cardboard, making four of each for each full arrow, and four flight feathers for each half arrow. Stick the tips and flights to the dowels using a quick-drying adhesive.

3 Insert the ends of the half arrows into the quiver as shown. Arrange the three full arrows on the surface of the cake, either lying across the top or stuck into the icing as if shot into the cake.

Finishing touches

With the quiver and arrows in place, wrap the edge of the cake with a wide scarlet ribbon, using a little royal icing to secure each end.

The laurel wreath decoration as shown consists of about 40 bay leaves (fresh or dried) sprayed with metallic paint. This is completely inedible, and if you prefer to produce the wreath from edible components, you can make the leaves from gelatin icing and paint them with gold food colour. The leaves can be simply fixed in position around the ribbon using small dabs of royal icing.

If you wish to produce a complete wreath that can be removed from the cake and kept as a memento of the occasion, you can make wired leaves as described for the Spring Cake on pages 68-69, colour them gold and attach them to a length of wire using florists' tape to secure them. The wire can then be wrapped around the cake and supported, if necessary, with cocktail sticks pushed into the sides of the cake.

As a final touch, we have sprinkled the top of the cake with tiny stars of gold foil. These are available from stationers or suppliers of decorative paper goods.

Alternatively, you could paint small stars on the blue-painted icing using gold food colour, or scatter a light dusting of gold lustre powder over the surface.

——PARTY DESSERTS——

The Sagittarian birthday, or any celebration throughout the year, provides an occasion for producing sumptuous desserts that both look and taste beautiful. We have included here three recipes for extra-special items for the party table.

KEY LIME PIE

1lb (450g) sweet pastry
14oz (450ml)/1¾ cups condensed milk
grated rind and juice of 2 limes
3 egg yolks
3 egg whites
4oz (125g)/½ cup caster sugar

Line an 8in (20cm) pie dish with sweet pastry, Cover it with lining paper and insert baking beans to weight the paper. Bake blind for 15 minutes at 400°F (200°C)/gas mark 6 with paper and beans in place, then for a further 5 or 6 minutes with the weights and paper removed. The pie shell should be cooked through and a pale golden colour. Let the shell cool completely before adding the filling.
Put the condensed milk into a bowl and add the egg yolks and the grated rind and juice of the limes. Mix together. (If you prefer, add the rind and juice of one lime and taste the mixture before adding more, to get the right degree of sharpness.)
Pour the mixture into the pastry shell and bake at 350°F (180°C)/gas mark 4 for about 25 minutes or until the filling is set. Remove from the oven and allow to cool.
Whisk the egg whites until they form stiff peaks. Add half the caster sugar and whisk again until the mixture is glossy and holds firm peaks. Fold in the remaining sugar and spread the meringue mix on top of the pie, sweeping it into swirls and peaks. Return to the oven, set fairly high, for a few minutes until the meringue is golden. Serve warm at room temperature or, if the pie is not to be eaten immediately, store in a refrigerator.

PAVLOVA

5 egg whites
10oz (300g)/1¼ cups caster sugar
2tsp (10mg) cornflour
½ tsp (2½ml) vanilla essence
1 tsp (5ml) malt vinegar
½ pt (300ml)/1¼ cups double cream, whipped
fruit to decorate

Preheat the oven to 300°F (150°C)/gas mark 2. In a large mixing bowl, beat the egg whites until they form stiff peaks. Beat in 4½oz (125g)/½ cup caster sugar and continue beating until the mixture is very stiff and glossy. Fold in the remaining sugar, then the sifted cornflour, and finally the vanilla essence and malt vinegar.
Pile the mixture onto a baking sheet covered in greaseproof paper or non-stick baking parchment and loosely shape it into an 8in (20cm) round. If you wish, you can pile half the mixture, then add swirls and rosettes applied with a piping bag and a large star-shaped nozzle. Place the baking sheet in the oven and bake for 1 hour. Turn off the oven and leave the meringue inside for a further 30 minutes, or until crisp on the outside and soft in the centre. Remove from the oven and allow to cool completely. When cold, lift off the baking sheet. You may need to slide a spatula underneath the meringue to loosen it from the paper. Place the meringue on a serving plate. Spoon the whipped double cream onto the meringue and decorate the Pavlova with fresh fruits to taste.
Note: The essential feature of a Pavlova is that is is crisp on the outside and has a superb marshmallow texture inside, by contrast with a meringue, which is crisp and crumbly. If the outer layer of your Pavlova cracks and collapses somewhat, simply use piped whipped cream to disguise any gaps and irregularities.

POACHED PEARS

8 firm pears
4oz (125g)/½ cup sugar
1pt (600ml)/2½ cups red wine
strip of lemon peel
piece of cinnamon

Using a saucepan in which the pears fit snugly, put in the wine, sugar, lemon peel and cinnamon and heat until the sugar dissolves. Boil the mixture for 5 minutes and then allow to cool slightly.
Peel and core the pears, stand them in the syrup, if necessary taking a thin slice off the bottom of each pear so that they stand up in the pan. Add more wine if necessary to cover the pears. Cover the pan with a lid and poach the pears gently until cooked through. This may take 25 to 45 minutes, depending on the variety and ripeness of the pears.
Allow the pears to cool until the syrup is tepid, then remove and drain the pears, arrange them in a serving dish and chill. Strain the syrup and boil to reduce, until thick. Add lemon juice or sugar to taste. To serve, turn the pears in the thickened syrup and stand them on a plate. Pour the remaining syrup around the pears. The pears are delicious with Chantilly cream (cream, sugar and vanilla). Alternatively, surround them with fruit purées made from raw or poached soft fruits sieved to remove any seeds.

53

THE SIGN OF CAPRICORN

This elegant dome of starry light makes a breathtaking spectacle that belies the simple process used for its construction. The dome is made from gelatin icing moulded over a hemispherical base (see below left). It is pierced all over with tiny holes but holds its shape exactly once dry. After colouring, the dome is positioned right over the cake, so that light from the single large candle on the cake filters through as a myriad stars. The cake and dome are elevated on columns above a baseboard ringed with small birthday candles. The many focused points of light on and around the glowing dome create a dramatically exciting centrepiece.

POP-UP CARDS

The thrifty but humorous Capricornian will appreciate a personalized handmade card that easily rivals the prettiness and invention of any commercially produced greetings card. Capricorns make loyal friends, and will be delighted by such a personal and thoughtful gesture. Decorated with the recipient's favourite colours, a beautiful flower, ribbon bow or butterfly motif immediately conveys your fond wishes for a happy birthday. These designs are based on simple paper cutting techniques that produce attractively sculpted effects very easily.

Creating the dome *The dome is moulded from gelatin icing smoothed over a large copper egg bowl (far left). Sections of ordinary drinking straws are used to punch holes in the icing (left) through which the candlelight from the cake casts a starry glow. The effect of the night sky and the Capricorn sign and constellation are painted on the dome with food colours.*

These examples show two types of pop-up card. The ribbon bow and flower border (above) are both made by cutting and scoring a single piece of heavy paper or thick card. For the tulip design (top) and butterfly motif (above), each card is made from two sections and intended to be displayed fully open. You can decorate the cards with colours in any way that you wish. Our designs include simple painted borders that add a neat finishing touch.

CAPRICORN

22 December-20 January

The sign of Capricorn is often represented by the strange image of a hybrid creature that is half goat, half fish. We have made this symbol one of the focal points of a dramatic design representing the heavenly firmament – a glowing dome of midnight sky studded with points of light on which the sign of Capricorn is traced in gold. This idea could, of course, be adapted to any of the signs of the zodiac. Although the overall design seems stunningly ambitious, the dome itself is quite easy to make and, of all our zodiac cakes, this is one of the most simple to construct. Much depends on the presentation: the cake is concealed beneath the dome, and both stand supported by a ring of decorative columns. Candlelight emanates from within and also surrounds the dome.

Because the cake is not seen, you can use any recipe for the cake and icing, to your own taste. As the overall design is quite large, we used a 10in (25cm) round fruit cake that would supply plenty of portions to feed a large party.

Artwork for the cake design to be found on page 126-127

FOR THE CAPRICORN CAKE
10in (25cm) round cake
14in (35cm) and 20in (50cm) round cake boards
14in (35cm) diameter mould (a large bowl or ball)
3lb (1.4kg) gelatin icing
drinking straws
food colours: gold (or gold marker pen), ice blue, berry blue, grape violet
flat-backed diamanté pieces (optional)
cake pillars
domestic candle or nightlight
birthday candles and holders
ribbons for edging cake boards

THE CAKE

Making the dome

The dome is made from gelatin icing, but we recommend that you do not attempt to eat it, simply enjoy the decorative effect. The icing is modelled over a hemispherical mould. We used a large copper egg-mixing bowl which is a perfect hemisphere measuring about 14in (35cm) across, which easily accommodates a 10in (25cm) cake. Since the icing dome is not intended to be eaten, you can use any suitable object as the mould. We suggest using a large beach ball, which will need to be firmly anchored to your work surface while you apply the icing and allow it to dry. For this you could use lumps of Plasticine, or a similar material that prevents the ball from rolling away as you work on it but is easily removable afterwards.

Such balls are usually made from two hemispheres welded together and have a visible seam around the centre, which can be the guide to trimming your hemisphere of icing. If you tie a string around the seam you will actually be able to feel it through the icing and it will clearly mark the level to which you should trim the hemisphere.

1 Begin by making up 2lb (900g) gelatin icing. This should be soft and pliable, so do not add too much icing sugar or cornflour, which would dry it out. Knead the icing and while it retains the warmth of your hands, roll it out on a surface lightly dusted with cornflour.

2 With hands lightly dusted with cornflour, lift the sheet of icing and lay it over the top of the bowl or ball acting as the mould. Smooth it out gently so that it perfectly follows the hemispherical shape.

3 Use a sharp knife to trim away the

excess icing at the base of the hemisphere. Leave the icing to firm up slightly.

4 Begin the process of decoration by cutting a circle about 1½in (4cm) in diameter at the top of the hemisphere. This will act as an outlet for the heat of the candle on the cake, so that the icing dome will not become singed inside.

5 Take a plastic drinking straw and cut it into 1in (2.5cm) lengths. Punch holes in the icing randomly all over the surface of the dome. These will create the starry effect when the candlelight shines through the dome. You can cut a lot of holes, as the icing will remain quite strong when dry.

6 Leave the icing in place on the mould at least overnight and preferably for 24 hours. Keep it in a warm, dry room; in a damp atmosphere it will not harden sufficiently. When the outside of the dome is completely dry, remove the shape from the mould and allow it to stand for several hours more so that the inside dries out completely.

Decorating the dome

There are two elements that make decorating the dome easier if the icing is not to be eaten. The first is using graphite paper to trace down the Capricorn design on the dome surface. The second is using a gold marker pen to go over the design and add the astrological signs and symbols that also appear on the dome. You may find it easier to control a marker than a brush on the curving surface. The gold colouring will repel the blue subsequently applied, leaving your design standing out clearly on the midnight sky effect. Alternatively, you can use gold food colour and a brush to paint the detail.

1 Replace the dried icing dome over the mould. Enlarge the artwork to the required size and trace the design onto the surface of the icing using graphite paper. Either repeat the Capricorn symbol around the sides of the dome or add any other suitable symbols, as preferred. When the drawing is complete, go over all the lines in gold.

2 Apply shades of blue food colouring all over the dome to make a gradated colour effect representing the sky. We used an airbrush to apply ice blue, berry blue and grape violet colouring, gently blending the colours into each other. Alternatively, you can use a sponge or a mist-sprayer to apply the colour with similar effects. Create swirling patterns of blended hues to give atmosphere to the design.

3 When the overall colouring is completely dry, add small gold dots at random over the surface to represent star clusters and constellations. For added sparkle, finish by sticking on flat-backed pieces of diamanté.

Assembling the decoration
To achieve the final effect, you need two cake boards, one to support the cake and dome and one to form the base of the design on which the candles and pillars stand. For our example, the upper board was 14in (35cm) in diameter, the lower one 20in (50cm). Small pillars are available from suppliers of materials for cake decoration. You can obtain white pillars and spray them in colours appropriate to the design, or use silver pillars which also look effective. As a finishing touch to the edges of the cake boards, we wrapped them around with a rich purple ribbon.
The cake carries a single domestic candle cut down to suitable height to fit within the dome, underneath the hole cut at the centre top. The candles around the edge of the cake board are typical small birthday candles. For a really spectacular effect, use many candles to create a generous ring of light around the dome. You can choose a symbolic number, rather than the actual number for the age of the birthday person. We used silver candle-holders with the bases cut down so they could be pushed firmly into an icing layer covering the lower cake board.

1 Place the cake with its single candle on the 14in (35cm) cake board. Position the dome over the cake and wrap the edge of the cake board with ribbon.

2 Roll out a sheet of gelatin icing and use it to cover the surface of the larger cake board. When dry, paint it in the same way as the dome, with a night-sky background and gold dots and diamanté pieces representing stars. Position the pillars on the iced board to form a ring about 12in (30cm) across. Place the small candles in their holder around the outer edge of the board, then finish the edges with ribbon.

3 Place the smaller cake board with the cake and dome on top of the ring of pillars. All that remains is to light the candle inside the cake and those around the edge of the larger cake board just before serving.

Timing
For the icing dome to harden, it needs to

be left overnight or for up to 24 hours, so you will need at least two days to complete the whole design.

——POP-UP CARDS——

Capricorns are known for being thrifty and prudent, but also for a characteristic sense of humour. Our designs for pop-up cards provide an opportunity to make something stylish and amusing, at little cost. These easily match any birthday card you could buy and a personalized greeting is sure to be appreciated.
Two of the designs – the ribbon bow and flower border – are based on the traditional pop-up method of cutting and scoring a single piece of paper or card in a way that makes the motif emerge from centre fold of the card when it is opened. The tulip and butterfly motifs are a little more complex. The motif is designed to stand up from the card when it is opened out flat. This involves dividing the card itself into two sections which are then assembled on a backing sheet.
The materials that you need include tracing paper for tracing and enlarging the design (see page 13), heavy paper or very thin card, a metal ruler, adhesive, and a scalpel or fine craft knife for cutting. For scoring the paper to make the folds the ideal instrument is a stylus, but it is possible to use the tip of a sturdy scissor blade, carefully handled. Scoring should break the tension of the paper or card so that it is easily folded, but the instrument should not actually cut the material.

Ribbon bow
Enlarge the artwork to the required size for your card. Cut along the outlines of the motif, leaving it attached to the card where shown. Score along the lines still attached to the card and score the centre fold of the card. Crease the folds along the edges and centre of the bow to push the motif outwards, then fold up the card. In our example we have painted the bow in shades of yellow and have added detail of the ribbon loops with fine silver lines.

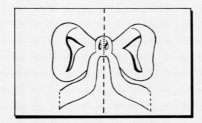

Flower border
Draw up the artwork on the card. Cut out the detail of the flower border and the centre section inside the border. Score and fold the card as shown. Paint the design and allow it to dry. Stick the card to a suitable coloured paper backing.

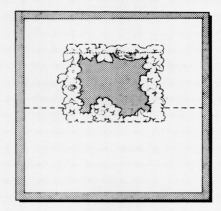

Butterfly
This card is made in two sections, cut as shown in the artwork. When you have cut out the shape, fold up the butterfly halves, bring the centre edges of the card together and slot the pieces together to make the full motif. Stick a backing sheet to the card to secure the centre line.

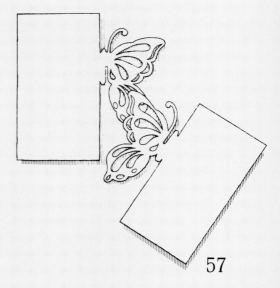

Icing the cake *Trace the design down on a piece of gelatin icing.*

Fill in the colour areas, blotting the damp colour to give it a faded tone.

Fix the fragment on a layer of royal icing and tap it to create hairline cracks.

THE WATER CARRIER

This evocative design is very simply achieved. The fragment is painted on a cut-out piece of gelatin icing and fixed to the cake with a layer of royal icing. The bold lines and clearly defined colour areas of the Egyptian-style image can be approached with confidence and, as all the painting is completed before the fragment goes on the cake, there is no chance of ruining the overall effect with a last-minute error. You can adapt the design to any size of square cake, according to the number of servings you require.

If necessary, retouch the surface of the iced cake to create the required texture.

MARBLED CAKE

This simple but effective idea can be applied to any birth sign. Here, the astrological symbol for Aquarius stands out in relief on a blue-marbled background resembling lapis lazuli. For each of the zodiac signs, you can create a similar effect using the appropriate symbol and a background coloured and textured like the birthstone attributed to the sign. The raised parts of the cake are created with marzipan layers and covered cleanly with fondant icing on which the colour is painted.

AQUARIUS

21 January-19 February

The design for the Aquarian birthday cake reinterprets the usual image of the Water Carrier. Most representations are loosely based on the styles of Greek or Roman art and show the Water Carrier as a male figure. In the cake decoration, we have taken our inspiration from Egyptian wall painting. The design is constructed as a fragment that might have survived from an ancient mural, and the figure is distinctly female. The clear lines of the Egyptian-style design make the process of painting it rather similar to that of colouring an image in a child's painting book, so this is a good opportunity to allow children to be involved in the preparation for a birthday party. Food-colour pens can be used rather than a paintbrush and liquid colours, and may prove more suitable for a young child. An alternative design for Aquarius, that can be easily adapted to any of the zodiac signs, is the marbled cake illustrated on the previous page. The silver flashes on top of the cake are the astrological symbol for Aquarius, standing out in relief against the rich blues and purples of the painted marbling. Whatever the birth sign you wish to represent, you may prefer the abstract representation of the symbol to the pictorial device traditionally associated with the sign (all of the twelve symbols are shown on the facing page). You can match this with painted effects related to the birthstone of the given sign.
Artwork for the cake design to be found on page 126-127

FOR THE WATER CARRIER CAKE

10in (25cm) square cake
8oz (225g) gelatin icing
royal icing made with 2 egg whites
food colours: light blue, dark blue, pink, brown

—THE WATER CARRIER—

Making the painted fragment

The design as illustrated is fitted onto a cake 10in (25cm) square, but you can adapt it to the size you require. For the size shown, you need 8oz (225g) of gelatin icing (see page 9).

1 Draw up the design to the required size and trace it onto a piece of paper or baking parchment.

2 Roll out the gelatin icing as thinly as possible. Place the design over the icing and, using a sharp knife or scalpel, cut around the outline of the design. Leave the piece of icing to dry for 10 or 15 minutes.

3 Put the drawing back over the icing piece and trace out the pattern with a cocktail stick, to make a light impression in the surface of the icing. Allow the icing to dry for at least two hours.

4 Mix up the various food colours that you wish to use. Then simply fill in the design with colour following the impressed outlines. To avoid smudging, work with one colour at a time and allow it to dry before starting on the next.

5 To create the slightly faded effect indicating the age of the fragment, blot the colour gently with tissue or kitchen paper while it is still wet.

6 Make a few small, irregular painted fragments that can be used to decorate the sides of the cake.

Fixing the fragment to the cake

The fragment of painted icing is fixed to the cake using royal icing. If you set the fragment in icing, as described below, you will have to cut the painting when serving the cake. If you prefer to not lose the design you can simply ice the whole cake with royal icing, allow it to dry, and lay the painted fragment on top, removing it before serving.

60

To prepare the cake, you need only cover it with marzipan in the traditional way, then ice it with royal icing. We suggest that you make up a quantity of royal icing based on two egg whites (see page 8), resulting in a stiff consistency that is still easily spread with a knife. It is not necessary to apply the icing perfectly smoothly, as some roughness and undulation in the surface adds to the effect of the design.

1 Spread royal icing on top of the cake to a thickness of about ¼ (6mm), or to your own taste.

2 Place the painted fragment in position and press down lightly to set it in the royal icing.

3 To create the effect of hairline cracks in the fragment, cover the icing piece with greaseproof paper and tap lightly at intervals all over the surface. (This stage is optional, if you prefer not to risk damaging your painting.)

4 When the top of the cake is complete, apply royal icing to the sides and press on a few smaller painted fragments.

FOR THE MARBLED CAKE

9in (23cm) round cake

2lb (900g) marzipan

1-1½lb (450-675g) fondant icing

food colours: light blue, dark blue, purple, silver

——MARBLED CAKE——

The basis of this design is a 9in (23cm) round cake covered with marzipan. The raised edge of the cake and the Aquarius symbol represented in relief at the centre are made with additional marzipan layers. The whole is then covered with a layer of fondant icing (see page 8) and painted with the marble effect. For this, we used an airbrush to lay the gradated tones of blue and purple, but you can get a similar effect using a fine mist-sprayer of the type used for spraying plants, or you can apply a slightly more textured effect of blended colours using a sponge.

1 Roll out 1lb (450g) marzipan into a sheet about ½ (1.2cm) thick. Using the cake tin in which you baked the cake as a guide, cut out a circle of marzipan 9in (23cm) in diameter.

2 Using a small plate as a guide, cut out a circle within the original circle, leaving a ring of marzipan about ¾in (2cm) wide. A precise width is not essential, but make

sure the inner circle leaves room at the centre for the symbol.

3 Lift the marzipan ring onto the top of the cake and use a little sieved apricot jam to make sure that it adheres to the marzipan layer covering the cake.

4 Roll out the remaining marzipan into a sheet about ½ (1.2cm) thick. Copy the Aquarius symbol onto greaseproof paper and use this as a pattern to trace the lines onto the marzipan, using a cocktail stick.

5 Cut out the symbol with a sharp knife or scalpel, keeping the edges as a clean and sharp as possible. Stick the symbol on the centre top of the cake, using sieved apricot jam to secure it.

6 On a surface lightly dusted with cornflour, roll out 1-1¼lb (450-565g) of fondant icing into a sheet large enough to cover the whole cake.

7 Lay the icing sheet over the cake and, with fingers lightly coated in cornflour, ease the icing over the raised design on the top of the cake. Make sure it stretches into all the detail - this may take some minutes. Smooth the icing down around the sides of the cake.

8 Trim the excess icing to the edge of the cake. Leave it for about an hour, until the icing is dry.

9 Apply gradated shades of blue and purple to the surface by spraying or sponging. Add detail using a paintbrush to form the blue and silver tracery of the marble veins. (See pages 34 and 42 for further detail on marbling.)

10 Decorate the Aquarius symbol as almost solid silver, with a little blue breaking through and dark blue edges emphasising the shapes.

-ASTROLOGICAL SYMBOLS-

Each sign of the zodiac has an astrological symbol as well as its more familiar figurative symbol, such as the Taurean bull and the Sagittarian archer. These symbols provide useful motifs for cake decoration, as in the marbled cake described on this page and the sugar panels decorating the Aries cake on page 18. There are also other associations for each sign that can provide decorative inspiration, particularly the element governing the sign, the birth stone and the preferred colours. These are listed below together with graphic representations of the symbols.

Aries the Ram
Element: Fire **Stone:** Diamond
Colour: Red

Taurus the Bull
Element: Earth **Stone:** Sapphire
Colours: Blues, greens, pink

Gemini the Twins
Element: Air **Stone:** Agate
Colour: Yellow, but Geminis love all colours

Cancer the Crab
Element: Water **Stone:** Pearl
Colours: Greys and greens

Leo the Lion
Element: Fire **Stone:** Ruby
Colours: Orange, golden yellow

Virgo the Maiden
Element: Earth **Stone:** Sardonyx
Colours: Dark shades of blue, grey and brown

Libra the Scales
Element: Air **Stone:** Sapphire
Colours: Pastel blues, pinks, mauves

Scorpio the Scorpion
Element: Water **Stone:** Opal
Colours: Dark reds

Sagittarius the Archer
Element: Fire **Stone:** Topaz
Colours: Purple, dark blue

Capricorn the Goat
Element: Earth **Stone:** Turquoise
Colours: Black and dark shades of grey, green and brown

Aquarius the Water Carrier
Element: Air **Stone:** Amethyst
Colours: Electric blue, and all shades of blue

Pisces the Fish
Element: Water **Stone:** Moonstone or bloodstone
Colours: Sea greens, blues and greys

FISH MOULDS

An elegant and detailed copper mould (right) does much of the work for you in shaping the attractive fishes filled with delicious chocolate truffle mix (below). Lining the mould with marizipan allows you to turn out the fish shapes cleanly. Then you cover them with fondant icing and add colour to enhance the detail. This is a quick and easy way to achieve an excellent result, especially as the truffle mixture requires no cooking. There are various shapes and patterns of kitchen moulds available, so you can adapt this idea to other designs for different occasions.

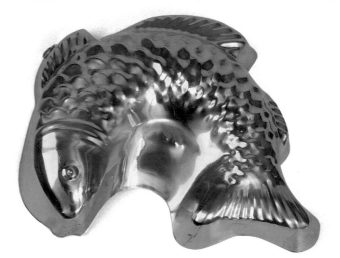

Making the fish mould *Roll out a sheet of marzipan and press it into the mould.*

Press the truffle mixture into the lined mould, packing it down gently but firmly.

Cover the moulded shape with fondant icing on which the colour can be applied.

LEAPING FISH

Two beautiful fish leaping through turbulent water (above) create a very detailed and elaborate effect, but the process of carving and decorating the cake is simpler than you may think. The basic shapes of the water and fish bodies are cut into the cake itself. The dorsal and tail fins are modelled in the marzipanning stage and the entire shape is covered with fondant icing before colouring.

FISH POOL

A stencil motif is used to form the two interlocking shapes of golden fish swimming in a calm pool that reflects the blue sky (right). The addition of a scattering of autumn leaves, formed out of gelatin icing, enhances the illusionistic effect of the design.

PISCES

20 February-20 March

The symbol of the fish suggests many wonderful ideas for cake decoration. We have included here three designs, each very striking and individual, that involve different levels of skill and effort. One is a painted design that can be applied either directly to the top of the iced cake or to a plaque of gelatin icing. The other two Pisces cakes are shaped before icing and colouring, one by creating the cake itself inside a decorative mould, the other by carving the basic cake before working on the decoration. All of these designs produce a spectacular finish, but you will find that none is as difficult to achieve as may appear at first sight.
Artwork for the cake design to be found on page 126-127

FOR ONE PISCES MOULD
fish-shaped kitchen mould
8oz (225g) marzipan
chocolate truffle mixture (see page 93)
apricot jam
8oz (225g) fondant icing
food colours: blue, pink, green edible silver lustre powder

PISCES TRUFFLE MOULDS

The cake consists of a rich chocolate truffle mixture that is very easy to make – it needs no cooking. For the recipe, turn to page 93. To form the shape of the fish you require a shaped baking mould, or two if you wish to make the two fishes at the same time. This is available from any good cookware shop or department store.

The truffle mixture is contained within a layer of marzipan first applied to the inside of the mould. The finished cake is iced with fondant icing (see page 9) to which the colours are applied.

1 Roll out 8oz (225g) marzipan on a surface lightly dusted with cornflour. Place the marzipan sheet inside the fish mould and gently press it into the detail. Trim the marzipan to the edge of the mould.

2 Spoon the truffle mixture into the mould. Press it down gently to pack the filling solidly into the mould. Level off the mixture, leaving a fine strip of marzipan at the edge of the mould.

3 Finely coat the surface of the truffle mixture with apricot jam. Roll out 8oz (225g) marzipan into a sheet large enough to cover the top of the mould. Lay it over the truffle mixture, trim the edges and press it to the uncovered marzipan strip around the top of the mould. Turn the cake out of the mould and allow it to dry for two hours.

4 Dust your work surface lightly with cornflour. Roll out 8oz (225g) fondant icing into a sheet large enough to cover the whole cake. Make the icing sheet as thin as possible so it will pick up the moulded detail of the cake. Lay the icing over the cake and smooth it gently over the detail. Trim the icing to the lower edge of the cake.

5 Mix up several shades of pale food colours – the example shown is decorated with blue, green and pink washes of colour. Brush the colours over the surface, merging them gently into each

other. Brush on some edible lustre powder to give a final shimmer to the fish scales and the eye.

FOR THE LEAPING FISH CAKE
three 10in (25cm) square sponge cakes
sieved apricot jam
2lb (900g) marzipan
1½-2lb (675-900g) fondant icing
food colours: berry blue, ice blue, rose pink, mint green
edible silver lustre powder
royal icing made with one egg white

LEAPING FISH

This three-dimensional cake is carved from three 10in (25cm) square sponge cakes stacked one on another. Use the main picture as a reference for following the steps for carving the cake. The method describes carving one fish on each side of the cake using a diagonal guideline. If you prefer, you can actually cut the cake in half diagonally and carve each part separately, then rejoin them before icing.

1 Take a sharp knife and score a diagonal line across the top cake in the stack. This forms a framework of two triangles within which you carve one fish on each side of the cake.

2 Pick out a point to form the nose of the upward-leaping fish close to one end of the diagonal line. Locate the tail fin at the other end of the diagonal and carve the cake downward, taking the level down by about two-thirds as you reach the tail.

3 Carve down and out in a curving swathe from nose to tail at the outer edge of the cake to create the line of the fish's body. Make a corresponding curve on the inner side, carving down and slightly outwards within the triangle created by the diagonal. Undercut the inner curve slightly to form the fish's belly. In effect, the final shape should look rather like a large, fat banana. You do not have to carve detail of the tail and fins, as these are added later with marzipan.

4 Carve the second fish in the same way as the first, but reversing the direction, so that the tail end is at the highest point and the nose is directed downward. When both fish are shaped, roughly carve the surrounding areas of cake to represent the turbulent water around the fish.

5 With the whole cake roughly shaped, stand back and check whether it requires refinement or detail. Proceed with any further carving in small steps, shaving the cake little by little with a sharp knife.

6 Apply a layer of sieved apricot jam to half of the cake. Roll out a large sheet of marzipan and drape it over one side of the cake, letting it hang in the area between the two fish. Gently mould the marzipan to the shape of the fish, creating a clean, unbroken surface. The marzipanning can be rougher on those areas of the cake that represent water, but the fish body should be smoothed out cleanly. Trim the excess marzipan.

7 Repeat the process to apply a marzipan layer to the other half of the cake. If you have trouble smoothing out the marzipan, try to concentrate any folds or creases in the areas around and between the fish, where they can be disguised as swirling water.

8 To create the fins, take a block of marzipan and cut two triangular pieces at least 1/4in (6mm) thick, with the base of each triangle about 3in (8cm) long and the other two sides roughly equal to a height of about 1 1/2in (4cm). These two triangles form the dorsal fins, one for each fish. Attach them to the fish using a little apricot jam to secure them.

9 Gather up the remaining marzipan and make the two tail fins. Cut the shape of the tail about 3in (8cm) long and 2 1/2-3in (6-8cm) wide at the widest part. Moisten the tail end of each fish with apricot jam and press the tail into place. Arrange each tail fin so that it appears to have a flicking motion. If the tail of the downward moving fish is unsupported, bend it round and allow it to rest on the part of the cake representing the water.

10 When the marzipanning is complete, leave the cake to rest for at least 12 hours to allow the fin details to harden before the icing is applied.

Icing and painting the cake
The colouring of the cake is very important to the final effect, but as with the carving, you are aiming for an impressionistic effect and there is little specific detail apart from the eyes and the gills. In our example the colours were sprayed on with an airbrush. A mist-sprayer will provide a similar effect, or you can apply a looser paint finish using a sponge or large paintbrush.

1 Before applying the icing, brush the fish, including the fins, with boiled water or, if you prefer, brandy or sherry, to make the marzipan tacky and receptive to the fondant icing.

2 Roll out 1 1/2-2lb (675-900g) fondant icing on a work surface lightly dusted with cornflour. Make a sheet large enough to settle over the cake, allowing for the indentation between the fish. You may need help in applying the icing to the cake.

3 Lift the icing sheet on your rolling pin and lay one edge of the sheet against one of the fish. Gently lift the icing over the cake and allow it to fold down between the two fish, then lift it again and cover the second fish.

4 Coat your hands with a light dusting of cornflour and gently smooth the icing over the shapes of the fish. Be careful that the icing does not break over the protruding dorsal fins or that the weight of the icing does not push the fins out of shape. Pay careful attention to getting the icing in place on the fins before smoothing it out over the body of the fish.

5 Press the remainder of the icing down over the area of cake representing the water. Here, the icing can have rough folds and curls suggesting turbulence. When complete, trim the icing to the edges of the cake and leave it for several hours before you begin colouring it.

6 Mix all the colours you need in separate saucers before you begin. The colours used in this example were berry blue, ice blue, rose pink and mint green. Using only the berry blue and ice blue, start to apply colour to the icing representing water. Apply the blues in patches and let them blend together.

7 To paint the fish, begin with a strip of rose pink on the belly, then above that immediately paint a strip of mint green. Use berry blue and ice blue on the back. Apply the colours rapidly so that they merge freely while still damp. Allow them to dry before adding detail.

8 Using a fine paintbrush, paint in the eyes and gills with berry blue. Give the fish a dappled texture by adding spots of berry blue down the back. Allow the colour to dry for at least one hour before the next step.

9 To define the fishes more clearly against the blue water, brush the fish bodies lightly with silver lustre powder. This also gives them a shimmering, wet look. Load the paintbrush with powder and apply spots of lustre between the spots of berry blue on the fish backs. Add lustre spots to the eyes to highlight them.

10 To finish off the effect of the foaming water, make up royal icing using one egg white (see page 9) and mix it to the consistency of double cream. Using your fingers, spread this unevenly over the water to create crests on the waves and ripples, but leave patches of colour showing clearly through the white icing. You can use the royal icing to disguise any imperfections in the fondant icing or colouring, but avoid applying it to the fish bodies, so that these stand out clearly against the water.

FOR THE FISH POOL CAKE

round cake, marzipanned and iced

card or acetate stencil

food colours: yellow, orange, red, blue

gelatin icing leaves (optional)

———FISH POOL———

The basis of this design is a stencil motif that can be applied either to the top of a fondant-iced cake or to a plaque of gelatin icing that can be laid over the cake top. Allow fondant icing to dry for 12 hours before applying the colour.

1 Using the artwork on this page enlarge the motif to the required size and trace it out on thin cardboard. Cut out the areas of the design that will receive colour. Make three or four pinholes through the edges of the stencil and pin it to the icing. It must lie completely flat on the surface.

2 Mix up all the colours that you need in a palette or in separate saucers. Load your brush with colour and blot off the excess dampness, then carefully brush the icing surface in the areas exposed by the stencil. If you are overlaying two or more colours, start with the lightest one and build to the darkest.

3 When all the colour is applied, remove the pins from the stencil and lift it carefully from the icing surface. If you wish, you can at this stage add more detail to the motif, painted freehand.

4 To create the background, use a mist-sprayer or sponge to apply soft patches of berry blue. If you are spraying the colour, cut the shape of the motif from cardboard and lay this over the fish you have already painted to protect them.

5 If you wish to add floating leaves, as shown in the illustrated example, cut these from gelatin icing and paint them in autumnal shades mixed from food colours. For further detail of making leaves, see the instructions for the Autumn Cake on pages 70 and 72.

65

CHAPTER 3

SEASONAL CAKES

Whatever your birth sign, your birth date is also represented by one of the seasons of the year. This can be, if you prefer, the theme of your celebration. Perhaps you are not particularly attracted to the way your birth sign is characterized – you may not like the image of the Ram or the Lion, for example – or you may not feel sufficiently skilled to attempt one of the Zodiac cakes. As an alternative, we have created decorative ideas for each of the seasons using relatively simple techniques that create very effective results. We have also chosen to use a tiered cake for each design, rather than a single cake on one level. Tiered cakes are usually associated with weddings and, perhaps, rather conventional types of decoration, but there is wonderful potential for using them in less formal and more lavish ways.

SPRING
The light, free appearance of this lavishly piped cake encapsulates the freshness of spring. For decoration, you can buy small posies of fresh violets or make your own from gelatin icing and paint them with the rich hues of these charming flowers.

SUMMER

The wealth of summer fruits makes simple but sumptuous decoration for the tiered cakes, glistening with a tempting apricot glaze. You can choose to slice the larger fruits or use them whole, varying the tastes, textures and colours.

67

SPRING AND SUMMER

For all the seasonal cakes, we have chosen the same arrangement to form the tiers – 12in (30cm), 9in (23cm) and 6in (15cm) cakes stacked American fashion, one on top of another, creating three levels.
The design for the Spring cake reflects the light and delicate beginning to each year, using pale, loosely piped buttercream icing contrasted with dark, fragile spring violets. These are made from gelatin icing and wired together to form small posies.
For the Summer cake, what else but a sumptuous display of summer fruits could so perfectly suit the mood? They not only look and taste wonderful, the smell is equally appetizing. As a delicious complement to the sharp freshness of the fruits, we have included layers of rich crème au beurre between the cake tiers.

FOR THE SPRING CAKE

12in (30cm), 9in (23cm) and 6in (15cm) round cakes
buttercream icing
piping bag with nos. 47, 30 and 24 nozzles
gelatin icing
food colours: violet, yellow, green
yellow stamens
florists' wire
purple florists' ribbon

SPRING CAKE

The lightness of the design derives from the decorative effect of the piped buttercream, but meticulous piping is not at all necessary - in fact, the looser the better - so do not be put off if your piping technique is less than perfect. If you are unsure, just practice for a few minutes before you begin work on the cake. Of course, the delightful thing about working with buttercream is that if it goes wrong, you can simply scrape it off and begin again.

1 Assemble the cakes one on top of another and spread buttercream all over the surface.

2 Fit your piping bag with a no. 47 nozzle and loosely pipe a basketwork effect on the sides of each cake, working from top to bottom.

3 Put a no. 30 nozzle, a large star tip, into the piping bag and pipe generous swirls around the top edge of each cake.

4 Use a smaller star tip, such as a no. 24 nozzle, to pipe loose swagging trailing down from the edges of each cake. Again, the emphasis is on free-flowing lines, so try to work uninhibitedly.

BUTTERCREAM ICING

4 oz (125g) butter (or soft tub margarine)
8oz (250g)/2²/₃ cups icing sugar
2 tbsp (30ml) evaporated milk or lemon juice
few drops vanilla essence
Cream the butter until soft. Beat in the sifted sugar a little at a time, adding the vanilla essence and sufficient milk or lemon juice to give a fairly firm but spreading consistency.

Making the violet posies
It is a nice touch to make the violets yourself out of gelatin icing, but if this seems too difficult or time-consuming you can simply buy small posies of fresh violets and put them on the cake just before serving.
You may be able to find a small cutter of a suitable shape for the flowers, but you can just as easily work with a cardboard template drawn to your own design. To complete the flowers and gather them into bunches, you need to equip yourself with some fine florists' wire and yellow stamens, as sold for making artificial flowers. The finishing touches are added with fine strips of violet-coloured florists' ribbon.

1 Draw the flower shape on stiff cardboard and cut a hole about ¼in (6mm) diameter in the centre of the shape.

2 Make up a batch of gelatin icing (see page 9). For each flower, you need a ball of gelatin icing about the size of a small grape.

3 Roll an icing ball between your finger and thumb, drawing it out to make a shape resembling a golf tee. Place the fatter end down on the work surface and press out the edges so that you have a flat circular base with a small stalk sticking up in the middle.

4 Position the template so that the stalk of icing sticks up through the hole at the centre of the flower. With a sharp knife, trace around the flower template to cut the icing to shape.

5 Turn the flower over and use the end of a paintbrush to draw lines from the flower centre up through the middle of each petal, rolling the brush slightly to create the effect of veins running through the petal centres. Gently bend the edges of the petals up or down to give the flower a natural form.

6 Attach a yellow stamen to a short length of florists' wire, tying them together with a small piece of sewing thread. Insert the wire through the flower centre and draw it down so that the wire comes out through the stalk on the underside of the petals and the yellow stamen sits neatly at the centre of the flower.

7 Make as many flowers as you need for the cake and allow the icing time to dry. To colour them, mix food colours into shades of purplish-blue and simply brush the colour onto the petals. Brush outwards, leaving the centre of the flower slightly paler than the petal tips. For a very natural effect, add alternating small strokes of dark purple and yellow fanning out around the stamen.

8 To surround the violets you can make green ivy leaves from gelatin icing, in the same way as the flowers are made but with the florists' wire running right through the centre of each leaf. To do this, make a ball of icing and push a wire through the centre. Lightly dust your work surface with cornflour, flatten the icing ball and cut the leaf shape with the wire inside forming the central leaf vein. Gently bend the edges of the leaf to create a natural effect. Paint the completed leaves when they are dry.

9 Wire the violets into small bunches, surrounded by leaves. Cut purple florists' ribbon into fine strips and run a knife edge along the ribbons to make them curl. Bind the posies with ribbon and position them on the iced cake.

FOR THE SUMMER CAKE

12in (30cm), 9in (23cm) and 6in (15cm) round cakes
crème au beurre
selection of fresh fruits
apricot jam

——SUMMER CAKE——

The only question is how to choose from the lavish selection of soft fruits that you can use to decorate the Summer cake. The secret of success is to buy the widest variety possible, with the emphasis on colour and texture. Berries of all kinds are particularly decorative, but for variation, add grapes, plums, apricots, kumquats - anything you can find that will enhance the tastes and colours. Although the cake is designed for a summer celebration, since there is now an excellent range of fruits available all year round you can adapt the design for any occasion.

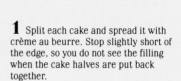

1 Split each cake and spread it with crème au beurre. Stop slightly short of the edge, so you do not see the filling when the cake halves are put back together.

2 Take a jar of apricot jam and push the jam through a sieve to remove all the fruit pieces, leaving a kind of purée. Thin this slightly with boiling water, or a mixture of water and a liqueur of your choice.

3 Take whole fruits or pieces of fruit, dip them in the glaze and arrange them around the bottom tier of the cake.

4 Decorate the second and third tiers of the cake in the same way. Allow the glaze to drip generously down the sides - for a really sumptuous, glistening effect, simply ladle any left-over glaze onto the fruit.

CRÈME AU BEURRE

4 egg yolks
4oz (125g)/½ cup sugar
⅙pt (100ml)/½ cup water
8oz (250g) butter
2 tsp (10ml) vanilla essence

Beat egg yolks lightly in a bowl until mixed. Heat sugar with water until dissolved. Bring to the boil until the syrup reaches the soft ball stage, 239°F (115°C) on a sugar thermometer. Gradually pour the hot syrup onto the egg yolks, beating constantly. Continue beating until the mixture is cool and thick. Cream the butter and gradually beat in the egg mixture, adding the vanilla essence.

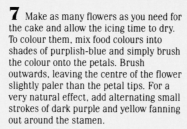

AUTUMN AND WINTER

The glossy chocolate coating provides a rich background for autumn leaves and berries made from gelatin icing. The design is most effective if you introduce a good range of colour variation, to catch the effect of autumn's gradual changes. Chocolate curls create a decorative woody texture contrasting with the smooth surface of the cake.

Sugar effects seem naturally to create the crisp sparkle of winter frost, snow and ice. Spun and poured sugar creating a fine network of frosted strands and jagged ice shards contribute a yellow tint that suggests pale winter sunshine glancing off the whiteness of the snow.

LEAF SHAPES

The more variation of shape and colour in the autumn leaves, the more natural the overall effect. You will find it is possible to cut even quite complex leaf outlines from gelatin icing if you use a fine, sharp blade. Delicate veining drawn on the leaf surfaces contributes to a detailed and convincing representation, together with carefully judged colour gradations in rich autumn shades. Curl the leaves in different ways to imitate the randomness of leaf fall.

AUTUMN AND WINTER

The contrast between the rich red-browns of autumn and the delicate frosted whites of winter further demonstrates how easily the same basic cake base can be given a completely different character and mood by easy techniques of decoration. The stacked arrangement of three different cake sizes is used as in the previous designs for spring and summer. The Autumn cake gets its deep chocolate sheen from poured ganache; for the Winter cake, the brilliant snowy covering is appropriately created from American frosting.

FOR THE AUTUMN CAKE

12in (30cm), 9in (23cm) and 6in (15cm) round cakes
chocolate ganache (two batches)
gelatin icing
food colours: orange, red, brown, green, purple
florists' wire
block of dark chocolate

——AUTUMN CAKE——

The chocolate ganache mixture is used in two ways. The cakes are first spread with cool ganache made in the traditional way to create a mousse-like texture. This seals the cake and forms a basis for poured ganache, which covers the entire surface of the tiered cake and contributes the glossy finish on which the autumn leaves are scattered.

1 Make up a batch of ganache and whisk it to a lightly moussey texture. You may need to double the quantities quoted in the recipe, as you are using the ganache both to fill each cake and to spread all over the tiered stack.

2 Split each cake and spread a filling layer of ganache. Put the cakes back together, assemble them in tiers and cover the whole surface of the stack with the remaining ganache. Ganache becomes more dense as it cools, so do not leave it for any length of time before you start to cover the cake. After covering, allow the cake to stand for an hour or more before proceeding.

3 Stand the cake on a cooling rack over a large plate. Make up another batch of ganache but do not beat the mixture to the lighter texture. Wait until the liquid ganache is tepid, with some warmth remaining, and then pour it over the top of the cake, making sure all the surfaces are covered. It should adhere quite easily to the cold ganache layer beneath. Allow the cake to cool before applying the decoration.

GANACHE

13oz (375g) dark chocolate
split vanilla pod
9 fl oz (250ml)/1 cup +2 tbsp double cream

Break the chocolate into pieces. Place it in a bowl and set in a warm oven to melt. Infuse the vanilla pod in the cream and bring to boil. Remove from heat and take out the vanilla pod. Gradually beat in the melted and slightly cooled chocolate. Beat vigorously until the mixture lightens and doubles in volume. Use immediately.

The leaf decoration

The leaves are made of gelatin icing cut to shape and painted in the same way as described for the ivy leaves on the Spring cake. You can use cutters or make your own templates to produce the right shapes, but be sure to vary the sizes and also, perhaps, the type of leaves. Form some of the leaves into curved and curling shapes and allow them to dry that way, to create the natural impression of fallen autumn leaves.

When colouring the leaves, keep in mind the autumn theme and bring in golds, reds and russets, representing green leaves that are turning colour and some that have completely changed to autumnal shades.

An additional feature that adds to the visual effect, though not strictly of the season, is small berries painted to look like blackberries in various stages of ripening. For each berry, just make a ball of gelatin icing, about the size of a hazelnut, and push a wire into it, then make a number of tiny icing balls and allow them to dry. Brush the large ball with royal icing or egg white, then stick the tiny balls all over the surface until you have something that looks like a blackberry.

Use different shades of red and black to paint the berries, giving a rich tonal effect. When they are complete, wrap the wires with green florists' tape and add the berries to the leaves decorating the cake.

Making chocolate curls

The final element of the Autumn cake is the crumbly chocolate curls interspersed with the autumn leaves. The effect of the curls depends on the temperature of the chocolate. If it is straight from the refrigerator, it will form a curl like a small, splintered thatch and you may wish to wait until the chocolate becomes less cold. Chocolate close to room temperature will provide large, loose curls. If the temperature is somewhere in between, the curls will be tight and clean.

1 Use a large block of good-quality dark chocolate. Melt it in a heatproof bowl, either by putting it into the oven until the chocolate melts, or by standing the bowl over a pan of simmering water.

2 Stir the chocolate to make sure there are no lumps. Using a pastry scraper or a large spatula, spread it evenly and very thinly on a baking sheet or marble slab. Put the chocolate in the refrigerator until it hardens.

3 Using a sharp metal scraper or a large carving knife, hold the blade at 45 degrees to the baking sheet and scrape off a strip of chocolate. This should curl as you scrape it. Repeat the process until you have as many curls as you need. If your preparation takes some time, refrigerate the curls until you are ready to use them.

FOR THE WINTER CAKE

12in (30cm), 9in (23cm) and 6in (15cm) round cakes
American frosting
poured sugar
spun sugar
holly leaves
cranberries, or other edible red berries

WINTER CAKE

All the elements of the Winter cake are specifically designed to add to the frosty effect, with ice shards of poured sugar emerging from the frosting and spun sugar representing frosty breath passing over the leaves and berries. The American frosting hardens crisply on the outside but remains soft underneath.

1 Make up a batch of American frosting. Assemble the cakes, including filling layers if you require them, and spread the frosting all over the tiered stack. Leave the cake to stand until the outer layer of icing hardens.

2 Make up a batch of poured sugar and pour it into a Swiss roll tin. A non-stick surface is best, but if you don't have one, brush the tin with a light coating of oil beforehand.

3 When the poured sugar is set, break it into uneven shards and push these into the frosting on each level of the cake.

4 Make up a batch of spun sugar and spread it around in small clumps and strands, creating a fragile network surrounding each tier of the cake.

5 Decorate the cake with holly leaves. You can make these from gelatin icing, but you may prefer to use real leaves as they have a lustre that an icing leaf cannot reproduce. Brush the leaves with egg white and sprinkle on caster sugar to complete the frosted effect.

6 As a finishing touch, add some red berries - not holly berries, of course, but perhaps cranberries or whatever similar fruit is available. The purpose is to add a flash of colour to the design.

POURED SUGAR

2lb 2oz (1kg) cube sugar
14 fl oz (435ml)/1¾ cups water
9oz (260g) glucose
food colour as appropriate

Pour the water into a pan and add the sugar. Stir gently. When the sugar has dissolved slightly, set the pan over a gentle heat and stir until the sugar has dissolved completely.
Once the solution bubbles, the sugar will throw out a kind of foam. Skim the surface to remove this, being careful to rinse the spoon each time so that you do not return any foam to the pan. Brush down the side of the pan with a pastry brush dipped in clean water to wash down the sides and prevent sugar crystals from forming, as these otherwise fall back into the pan causing further crystallization.
Add the glucose and stir it into the sugar solution. Cover the pan and turn up the heat. Place a sugar thermometer in the solution. Add food colour when the temperature reaches about 284°F (140°C). When the temperature reaches 312°F (150°C), take the pan from the heat. Allow the solution to stand for about 1½ minutes before pouring.

SPUN SUGAR
(Angel hair)

8oz (250g)/1 cup sugar
¼pt (150ml)/¾ cup corn syrup
2 tsp (10ml) pure beeswax

Combine sugar and corn syrup in a saucepan. Mix well and place on medium heat. Do not stir again. Bring to the boil and cook for about 12 minutes on medium to low heat until the sugar turns to a very pale ivory colour. This should be about a 330°F (160°C) on a sugar thermometer. If sugar crystals form on the side of the pan, brush down the sides with a pastry brush dipped in cold water.
Remove the sugar from the heat and add 2 teaspoons of grated pure beeswax. The pieces will melt straight away and mix into the sugar. (The wax has the effect of coating the sugar threads, making them "dry" and smooth, ensuring that they do not stick together or collapse.)
Let the syrup cool for a couple of minutes. Placing the pan in a bowl of cold water helps this process. Using two forks held back to back, dip the tines of the forks into the syrup and lift. The syrup should be thick.
Position a wooden rolling pin or length of dowelling extending well beyond the edge of the work surface. Weight down the end on the surface. Place sheets of newspaper on the floor beneath. Dip both forks into the syrup and move them over the rolling pin in a long, wide arc, so that long, thin threads of sugar are pulled and have time to solidify in the air. You may need to stand on a chair to give the necessary height.
When complete, slide the threads off the rolling pin and either use them immediately or store them in an airtight container.
(Note: Corn syrup, an American product, is available from some well-stocked food stores in the UK. If not, substitute liquid glucose, available from most chemists.)

AMERICAN FROSTING

1lb (450g)/2 cups granulated sugar
¼pt (150ml)/⅔ cup water
pinch of cream of tartar
2 egg whites

Pour the sugar and water into a large, heavy-based saucepan. Heat gently until the sugar has dissolved. Add the cream of tartar. Insert a sugar thermometer and bring to the boil. Boil to a temperature of 240°F (115°C).
Beat the egg whites until very stiff. Pour the sugar syrup in a thin stream onto the beaten egg whites, beating continuously. Continue beating until the frosting is thick enough to stand in peaks with the tips just tipping over. Quickly spread the frosting over the cake.

CHAPTER 4

EASY CAKES FOR NON-DECORATORS

When you are preparing for a party and have a million-and-one things to do, you may not be able to spare the time or concentration to create an ambitious or elaborate cake design. Or, if you are a newcomer to cake decoration, you may not feel sufficiently confident of your new skills to attempt one of the more complex zodiac designs. This section includes several cakes that demonstrate how an eye-catching and delicious centrepiece for your party table can be easily achieved with minimum skills or in a short space of time. We have chosen cakes and decorations of very different appearance, so that the selection contains something for everyone and may also inspire you to create your own simple but effective designs.

STRAWBERRY CAKE

Creating a beautiful confection should be a pleasure, not a chore. If you have not yet acquired confidence in the skills required for modelling or painting cakes, you may prefer to make a cake that is simply beautiful in itself. You need only follow the quick and easy recipe to create this sumptuous layered strawberry cake. When cut into slices, the meringue-covered cake reveals a light yellow sponge interior, slashed through with glistening strawberry pieces on a bed of whipped cream.

SKIER IN SNOWDRIFT

This witty image seems quite elaborate at first sight, but it is an appropriate choice for a beginner in cake decoration, as it creates a lively impression of the scene without too much detail. There is some basic carving involved in creating the underlying shapes of the fir trees and snowdrift, but the icing technique can be loose and inexpert, as any roughness adds to the effect of churned-up snow where the skier has come to grief. The skier himself becomes a curiously abstract combination of shapes simply modelled from marzipan.

Modelling the trees Carve small cakes into rough cone shapes fitting one on another.

Marzipan the cakes and drape them loosely with fondant icing, trimming to shape.

Paint rough shapes of deep leaf green to show foliage breaking through the snow.

MAKING IT
EASY

The two cakes illustrated on the previous pages show two quite different approaches to achieving a decorative result by easy methods.
In the first example, it is the textures and colours of the cake itself that provide the eye-catching effect. The summer strawberry cake is simply beautiful in itself and delicious to eat. The glorious colour scheme of pale gold, ivory, white and red is a direct result of the ingredients – no additional decoration is necessary, but for a finishing touch to decorate the cake stand we added a rich damask red Tudor rose, which also introduced a delightful perfume, with a spray of dark green leaves and bright rose hips. On top of the cake we scattered a few blackberries in various stages of ripening, to complement the vivid red of the strawberries.

The second cake is a humorous representation of a skier unfortunately crashed into a snowdrift and half-buried. It illustrates a theme that we had originally considered for the Sagittarian birthday – that it is sometimes better to travel hopefully than to arrive! In making this cake you can practise simple skills of carving and modelling, but the design deliberately incorporates the loose effect of the tumbled snow, so that none of the modelling or icing need be very precise. If you have little experience in shaping and decorating a cake, you will be delighted to find how easily you can recreate this witty and attractive scene.

SUMMER STRAWBERRY CAKE

2oz (60g)/¹⁄₄ cup butter (softened)
4oz (125g)/¹⁄₂ cup caster sugar
¹⁄₂ tsp (2¹⁄₂ml) vanilla essence
4 egg yolks
4oz (125g)/³⁄₄ cup plain flour
1 tsp (5ml) baking powder
3 tbsp (45ml) milk

FOR THE MERINGUE:

4 egg whites
8oz (250g)/1 cup caster sugar
small handful flaked almonds

Pre-heat the oven to 350°F (180°C)/gas mark 4. Prepare and line two 8in (20cm) round cake tins.
Cream the butter, sugar and vanilla essence until light and fluffy. Add the egg yolks one by one, beating between each addition. Sift the flour and baking powder, and fold them in lightly but thoroughly, alternating with the milk. Divide the mixture between the two tins.
To make the meringue, beat the egg whites until stiff and gradually add the sugar. Divide the meringue between the tins and sprinkle the surface of one cake with the flaked almonds.
Bake for 40-45 minutes. Turn the cakes out onto a wire rack to cool, meringue side down. Sandwich the cakes together with a generous layer of whipped cream and sliced strawberries. Finish with a light dusting of icing sugar.

FOR THE SKIER CAKE

14in (35cm) square cake board
two 8in (20cm), two 6in (15cm) and three 4in (10cm) round cakes
sieved apricot jam
3lb (1.4g) fondant icing
royal icing made with 1¹⁄₂ egg whites
2-3oz (50-60g) gelatin icing
two wooden barbecue skewers
food colours: red, blue, green, silver

SKIER IN SNOWDRIFT

The basic components of this design are two 8in (20cm) round sponge cakes, two 6in (15cm) and three 4in (10cm) cakes. This does seem to be a lot of cake, but the finished item amply caters for your party guests. Some of the cake is carved away in shaping the trees and snowdrift, but the offcuts need not be wasted.
The cakes are sealed and covered with marzipan – you will need about 3lb (1.4kg) – and iced with fondant icing and royal icing (see recipes on page 9). The base for the design is a 14in (35cm) square cake board.

1 Roll out 1lb (450g) fondant icing to a sheet large enough to cover the cake board. Lay it over the board and trim the icing to the board edges.

2 Place the two 8in (20cm) cakes one on the other and roughly carve away the edges to create a basic shape for the snowdrift. This should just form a simple, irregular mound.

3 Take one 6in (15cm) cake and carve it into a cone shape with a flat top to form the lower tier of the fir tree. Draw a small circle in the top with a sharp knife, about 1-1¹⁄₂in (3-4cm) from the edge. Then insert the knife blade into one edge of the circle with the blade tip emerging at the

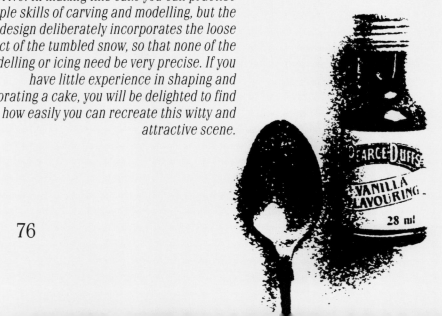

bottom edge of the cake. Cut right around the cake, keeping the knife at the same angle.

4 Carve the second 6in (15cm) cake into a cone with a pointed top, this time angling the knife from the centre top to the edge of the base when cutting.

5 Carve the three 4in (10cm) cakes in the same way to make two flat-topped conical tiers and a pointed cone for the top tier.

6 Position the snowdrift cakes on the iced cake board. Cover them with a thin layer of sieved apricot jam. Roll out 1lb (450g) marzipan and cover the cake with the marzipan sheet. Allow some irregularity in the marzipan layer, to give the roughened effect of the snowdrift.

7 Spread the carved cakes forming the two fir trees with sieved apricot jam. Roll out about ½lb (225g) marzipan and drape the marzipan sheet over the lower tier of the first tree. Let the marzipan fall into a "pleated" effect down the sides of the cake. Trim the lower edges. Gather up the remaining marzipan, roll it out and drape it over the pointed cone forming the top tier of the tree, again allowing it to flow into folds and creases.

8 Cover the sections of the three-tier cake in exactly the same way, marzipanning each tier separately.

9 To ice the trees, roll out fondant icing and drape it over the cake sections in turn, allowing it to form rough shapes and textures representing the tree branches. Use fondant icing in the same way to cover the snowdrift, then assemble the trees beside it on the cake board.

Adding colour and texture
To give the snow a blue tint, we applied blue food colouring using an airbrush. You can do this with a mist-sprayer if you haven't an airbrush or, if you prefer, you can leave the snow pure white. The trees are finished in two stages as follows:

1 Mix up a deep leaf green food colour and paint the whole surface of each tree.

2 Make up a batch of royal icing using 1½ egg whites to make a thick consistency, like double cream. Apply royal icing to the fir trees to create the impression of a fall of snow coating the branches. You can use a paintbrush or a knife. Load the edges of each tier of the tree and make irregular snow patterns over the green.

At the same time, use your fingers to apply royal icing loosely to the snowdrift, indicating the impact of the skier's crash.

Modelling the skier
Colour 8-12oz (225-350g) marzipan with red food colour. Use paste colour to create a strong tone. Split the marzipan into one large piece and two smaller pieces each the size of a walnut.

1 Form the larger piece of marzipan into a rounded pear-shape. Gently push it down onto the work surface to flatten the base. Model the base into the shape of the skier's buttocks and form the upper part into the lower back of the skier. Fix the shape to the side of the snowdrift and surround it with some roughly applied royal icing.

2 Take the two smaller marzipan pieces and fashion each one into the shape of a boot. It is not necessary to worry about the detail, just make a general boot shape. Place the boots upside down on each side of the skier and surround them with a roughened layer of royal icing.

Making the skis and ski-sticks
Make up a batch of gelatin icing and take out about 2-3oz (50-60g), saving the rest for another project.

1 Roll out the gelatin icing into a thin sheet and cut two lengths about 6in (15cm) long and ½in (1.2cm) wide. Shape one end of each ski into a point and make a small rest underneath, using a cotton wool ball or similar, so that the pointed tip turns upwards. Leave them to dry for several hours.

2 Take two 6in (15cm) bamboo skewers and paint them silver or red, as you prefer. Cut two circles out of gelatin icing and allow them to dry slightly, then thread them onto the skewers to form ski sticks. Allow to dry.

3 When dry, paint the skis and the icing circles on the ski sticks with silver food colour. Fix the skis to the skier's boots with a little royal icing. Plant the ski sticks in the snowdrift, sticking out at odd angles from the skier.

Alternative designs
This design shows how you can produce a witty and attractive decorated cake without too much expertise and it gave us several ideas about how this approach could be applied to other subjects. For example, if you were making a cake for someone with a passionate interest in rugby or American football you could create a scrum of chubby legs and bodies

fashioned roughly from marzipan in the same way that the skier's body and boots are made, perhaps with one head sticking out from the top of the scrum. You could also adapt it for someone interested in horse racing or show jumping, to show a large brush or tree where the rider has been thrown from the horse, with the jockey's rear end sticking out of the bush and perhaps a fox sitting nearby laughing at the spectacle. In this way you can see how a subject can be interpreted without necessarily including a great amount of detail, yet it effectively conveys the essential idea.

Using cake offcuts
When you have carved a cake for decoration, there is no need to waste the cut-off pieces. Sponge cake can easily be incorporated into a trifle or fruit dessert, but don't feel that you can only do this with plain sponge. Chocolate or devil's food cake offcuts also work well in trifle, perhaps with pears as the fruit and a chocolate mousse layer instead of the usual custard topping.
Offcuts of fruit cake cooked in a little melted butter make a delicious hot dessert. You can build madeira offcuts into a baked alaska, inside an earthenware dish. There are many such ways that you can use up left-over cake pieces, but you might prefer simply to put your feet up and enjoy them with a cup of tea.

HARVEST CAKE

Simple, well-considered decoration makes a plainly baked cake appear to be a generous feast. The colour of the cake is echoed in the warm gold and brown tones that form the scheme of the decoration — glacé fruits, ears of grain and attractive honeycomb-textured candles.

FAN CAKE

A patchwork of coloured marzipan stands out against a framework of elegant accessories. Strong colours and clean, geometric shapes create a dramatic presentation very different in character from traditional styles of cake decoration. The technique of decorating the cake top with marzipan hexagons is as easy as it could possibly be. The selection of precisely the right combination of design components — all very simple and inexpensive items — is the key to success.

BLUE-RIBBON CAKE

Ribbons and fresh flowers always create a charmingly decorative effect, but this design (right) finds a new way with traditional styling by using broad ribbon of a deep, rich blue in association with beautifully fragile flower sprays. Ribbon insert work quickly transforms a small, smoothly iced cake into an elaborate centrepiece.

78

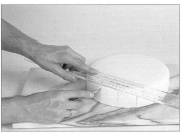

Applying the ribbon *Using a sharp scalpel, make clean incisions in the icing at regular intervals around the cake.*

Fold the ribbon and crease it sharply at intervals twice as large as those between the incisions on the cake.

Insert the ribbon folds into the incisions in the icing, forming a generous ruff of looped ribbon all around the cake.

79

SIMPLY SPECTACULAR

The three cakes illustrated in this section demonstrate in their different ways how easy it can be to achieve elegant and eye-catching decoration. The first design takes the warm brown colour of the cake itself as the starting point. Merely by adding a few extra ingredients and finishing touches, even the plainest cake can be given a specially rich appearance. The striking effect of the fan cake depends on a simple, bold colour scheme and careful placing of attractive accessories. The hexagonal chequerboard effect is created by one of the most basic techniques for covering a cake – the application of marzipan, in this case coloured and cut to shape. The very pretty, traditional style of the blue-ribbon cake is a perfect example of something that appears quite elaborate but requires no great skill on the part of the decorator – a quick and easy method produces this charming effect.

HARVEST CAKE

The general theme of this decoration is autumnal colours, tastes and scents. The cake that we chose to decorate is a chocolate almond cake, delicious to taste and pleasing in colour, but uneventful in appearance. You could equally begin with a basic sponge or fruit cake full of rich brown tones that can be complemented by decorative elements similar to the ones we have used here. To give lustre to the surface of the cake, we painted the top with apricot glaze.

The base on which you display the cake can make an important contribution to the overall impression. We looked for something appropriate to the theme and, rather than use a cake board or china plate, we chose a bread board with a lovely aged effect of colour and texture.

To begin with, we simply placed the cake on the board and wrapped it around with a deep, russet-brown ribbon.
The country harvest theme was developed in all the additional decorative elements. The ears of corn and wheat formed a natural complement to the earthy browns of the cake and board. Instead of attempting to incorporate the number of candles appropriate to the birthday, we chose to use just two, of different height and thickness. These have a particularly beautiful perfume and texture. Interestingly, each candle was made from a sheet of wax moulded on a honeycomb pattern, rolled to form the candle shape with the honeycomb on the outside.

As the finishing touch, we bought a selection of glacé fruits in a range of shapes, sizes and wonderfully subtle autumnal colours. These were simply arranged on the top of the cake and to form a small cluster at the side. The overall effect of the finished cake is of a very wholesome but appetizing confection.

FAN CAKE

This design uses just a few basic elements, combined in a way that creates a remarkably dramatic impact. Our colour scheme of red, black and white can be relied upon for a striking image, but you could of course devise an alternative scheme in your own favourite colours.

The only decoration actually applied to the cake consists of hexagonal shapes cut out of three colours of marzipan and assembled to form the pattern on the cake top. It is very easy to cut straight-sided hexagons, but when put together they form a much more complex pattern effect than squares and are a better complement to the shape of a round cake. We used a hexagonal biscuit cutter, which makes the process very simple, but if you don't have one and can't find one to buy, you can quickly make a template out of stiff cardboard and use it as a guide to cutting with a knife. Then, proceed with the marzipan decoration as follows:

1 Divide your marzipan into three batches, leave one white and colour the others black and red. Roll out each colour into a sheet about ¼in (6mm) thick, or to your taste, and cut a number of hexagons from each colour.

2 When you assemble the hexagons on the cake, the principle to remember is that a hexagon of one colour is always completely surrounded by hexagons of the other two colours – there are never two of the same colour side by side. Before you begin, cover the top of the cake with a thin layer of apricot jam, to act as an adhesive for the marzipan. Then, starting at the centre of the cake, position the hexagons one by one to form the patchwork pattern.

3 When you complete the design you will find that some of the hexagons hang over the edge of the cake. There are two ways to trim them neatly. The first is to use a pair of sharp scissors to cut close to the edge of the cake. Alternatively, you can turn the cake upside down and use a flat-bladed knife to trim the excess marzipan. This has the advantage that the weight of the cake on the marzipan prevents you from accidentally pulling off the pieces that should remain on the cake.

4 To finish the cake decoration, wrap the side of the cake with a broad, bright ribbon in one of the colours of your scheme.

As with the previous design, we wanted a base for the cake that would be completely in harmony with the theme and we were determined to find something of an intense, glossy black. An inexpensive black serving plate proved to be the perfect item. Here again, you can choose anything you wish as a suitable form of display base – a lacquered plate or tray, for example, could make a beautiful contribution to the design. Since this is intended to be a birthday cake, we naturally wanted to include candles. However, especially for an adult when you might need a large number of candles to represent the correct age, we suggest that a symbolic number of candles is more appropriate and creates a more elegant visual impact. We chose long, tapered red candles and placed three in a line at the back of the cake, so

that the eye is swept upwards through the design.
The final touch in this instance was provided by two inexpensive paper fans. The red fan, fully opened and propped against the back of the cake, provides a dramatic backdrop. The white fan, half-opened and laid in front of the cake, completes the framework of the design.

——BLUE-RIBBON CAKE——

This design is based on the traditional-cake decorating technique of ribbon insert work. Usually, this involves pushing short lengths of ribbon into incisions in the icing of the cake, giving the impression that the ribbon is threaded in and out of the icing all the way around.
In traditional cake-making, there is a tendency to work in miniature, using very fine ribbon, and although the effect is pretty, it gives no sense of scale. However, the technique is simple but effective, so we have adapted it to working with wide ribbon that allows you to achieve an impressive result very quickly. The ribbon decoration makes a small cake appear much larger, turning it into a worthy centrepiece for a birthday celebration.
The cake is an 8in (20cm) round sponge, which has been marzipanned and iced in the traditional way. Having decided to use a rich, deep blue ribbon, we gave the icing a faintly creamy tone that creates a very brilliant contrast. The ribbon is of the papery kind that florists use for decorating formal bouquets. It is 2in (5cm) wide, and you require 5-6½ft (1½ -2m) for this size of cake. This should include enough for decorating the posy on top of the cake.
The icing on the cake should be quite firm when you begin applying the ribbon, so leave it to dry for about 12 hours after icing. The technique for applying the ribbon is as follows:

1 With a sharp scalpel, make an incision in the icing on the side of the cake from 2in (5cm) above the base running vertically down to the base. Make similar incisions at 2in (5cm) intervals all around the cake.

2 Take the paper ribbon, measure off about 4in (10cm) and make a firm fold in the ribbon at that point. Crease the

ribbon sharply along the fold, as this will subsequently be inserted into the incision in the icing. Continue along the length of the ribbon making sharply creased folds at 4in (10cm) intervals. Fold the ribbon in the same direction each time.

3 Push the first ribbon fold into an incision on the side of the cake. If the incision is accurately cut to the same depth as the ribbon, it should hold the ribbon firmly in place. If it will not fit, gently extend the incision with the scalpel.

4 Insert the next ribbon fold into the next incision on the cake. Continue in this way until you have encircled the whole cake with loops of ribbon. To finish off, fold the final piece of ribbon into the original incision.

To create the lacy effect around the cake, we cut small sprays of white gypsophila and tucked them into each ribbon loop. Finally, we added a posy of snowdrops and ivy leaves, bound with curling strands of cut ribbon, as decoration for the top of the cake. It creates a very charming effect to keep to such a simple, fresh colour scheme, but you can choose small-scale floral decoration according to what is available at the time of year and you might wish to introduce another colour. To complete the presentation, we displayed the cake on an elegant glass cake stand.

CHAPTER 5

GIFTS WITH THE PERSONAL TOUCH

However enthusiastically you set off on a shopping trip to buy birthday presents, cards and wrappings, sometimes the perfect item proves totally elusive, or you may find that the cost of beautiful packaging almost exceeds the value of the gift. The answer to giving something special, personal and delightfully well-presented may lie in making both the gift and its wrapping yourself. In the following pages we offer ideas for charming personalized gifts and attractive and inventive packaging. We have devised a way of incorporating practical items relating to a person's hobbies or special interests into a decorative wreath that can be kept as an ornamental garland or dismantled so that all the objects can be used. You will see how this idea can be easily adapted to suit all tastes and interests. Edible gifts are always welcome, and we include recipes for delicious and unusual food items that can be attractively presented with a few special finishing touches. Our ideas for gift wrappings and packaging range from simple cards and envelopes made from layers of lovely papers to sculptured boxes and bags

DECORATIVE WREATHS

The idea behind each of these wreaths is to produce an attractive personalized gift that can be kept whole as a hanging decoration or can be dismantled so that all the components can be put to practical use. We have chosen three themes selected from popular pastimes – gardening (top), cooking (above) and sewing (right) – and have assembled a variety of inexpensive items related to these interests. The objects are wired or tied to a simple wicker or bent wood wreath to create a highly ornamental and unusual presentation. Ribbons and natural materials such as dried flowers and leaves for the gardener, spices and herbs for the cook, put the finishing touches to the decorative effect.

EDIBLE GIFTS
The true pleasure of gifts intended to be eaten lies not only in the delicious content of the foods but also in thoughtful and attractive packaging. Peaches and apricots in brandy (right) and richly coloured herb and fruit vinegars (below) are contained in beautifully shaped storage jars and bottles, with handwritten labels and ribbon decoration. Bouquet garni and sachets of spices for mulled wine (below right) are cleanly and prettily presented.

83

DECORATIVE GIFTS

A gift that you have made has a specially personal touch. Following the ideas in these pages, you can easily create highly personalized gifts that are both beautiful and practical and that will be enjoyed long after the birthday celebrations are over. One approach to giving a unique and individual present is to make something good to eat and to deliver it attractively packaged. We have included here a variety of recipes for edible gifts with unusual flavours – glossy preserved fruits, piquant herb and fruit vinegars, and fragrant bouquet garni. These form a tempting selection from which you can select the items best matched to the tastes of the recipient.

As a completely different approach to personalized presents, we have created decorative gifts that cater to the particular interests of the individual. Three beautiful wreaths represent a range of hobbies and pastimes, but we have chosen to focus on three themes – cooking, needlecrafts and gardening – to show how objects with evident practical value can be incorporated into an attractive hanging decoration that forms a unique gift.

—DECORATIVE WREATHS—

The decorative potential of the traditional wreath has been more fully exploited in recent years. Hanging decorations are considered equally appropriate for elegant, formal settings and for all kinds of informal celebrations. Each of our designs incorporates a number of inexpensive and easily obtained individual items that together add up to a highly ornamental presentation. The wreath can be kept and appreciated for its decorative value or can be taken apart so that the practical aspect of the gift items can be enjoyed.

The basis of each wreath is a simple wicker or bent-wood circle. You will find ready-made examples available from garden centres or in stores catering for the gift and decoration markets. Typically these wreaths are quite large and beautiful in themselves, and are not very expensive. Alternatively, you might make the wreath yourself by twisting and binding cane or wicker, or you could create a simpler version using strong wire wrapped around with an attractive fabric or interlaced ribbons.

All that remains is to choose the theme based on the hobby or leisure interest of the recipient and to obtain a number of small, colourful and useful objects relating to the theme that can be arranged to decorative effect. These can be attached to the wreath using wire, strong thread or double-sided tape, according to their shape and weight. Collect together all the items that you intend to include in the decoration before you actually wire anything in place. It is always a good idea to play with the elements to find how each item relates to the others and how they can be formed into a satisfactory design. If you have a lot of small items, as in the cook's wreath, it may be advisable to wire them together in bunches before attaching them to the wreath. For example, we wired together the bunches of cinnamon sticks, dried roses and some of the smaller implements before fixing them in place. This tends to make the decoration more robust.

Finally, although this may seem obvious, if you have a basic element creating a framework to the design, such as the paper ribbon wound around the cook's wreath or the tape measure in the needlecraft wreath, put this on the wreath first. It is difficult to thread tape or ribbon through the design once you have wired other elements in place.

——THE GARDENER'S—— WREATH

This design has the rather dramatic touch of the gardening hat that forms a focal point of the design. The gift might be intended to provide your gardening friend with a new hat, but you could alternatively "borrow" a favourite hat already in use.

We have added gardening gloves, a small garden fork and some pretty packets of seeds, decorated with dried leaves and flowers to complete the effect. If you wish to use fresh flowers, you can apply to the wreath small pieces of soaked florists' foam, wrapped in metallic foil to prevent dripping or seepage, and the stems of the flowers can be pushed into the foam. The colour scheme in this design is deliberately muted, based mainly on greens and yellows, but if your gardener likes to produce flowerbeds that are a riot of colour you can introduce more brightly coloured objects, or add ribbons and fresh flowers to produce a very vivid and lively impression.

—THE COOK'S WREATH—

For the keen or aspiring cook, a collection of useful wooden implements creates an attractive montage blending beautifully with natural dried flowers, grains and spices.

A major feature of this decoration is the large elaborate bow, which is made out of paper ribbon. This material can be found in well-stocked department stores or in retail outlets that specialize in dried flowers and accessories, or may be available from florists. When you buy the ribbon it looks rather like a coil of rope. As you unwind the coil, the paper ribbon spreads into a rich, crinkly mass. You will find this product invaluable for all sorts of decorative applications – it comes in some beautiful colours and behaves just like ribbon.

After tying this ribbon into a generous bow, we wound it around the wreath to form a basis for the remaining decoration. This was composed of a combination of old and new items. We found a set of wooden spoons dating from the Victorian period, and added to these new, inexpensive items including a lemon squeezer, a pastry wheel, a honey dip and a small rolling pin. To "age" the new wooden implements, we rubbed them with oil. The spoons were first applied to the wreath, attached with small pieces of wire, and the other items were added one by one, in a rather haphazard way, to create an interesting design.

The wreath was then filled out with

cinnamon sticks, dried corn, nutmeg and mace and dried roses. You could add anything here that is both decorative and of particular interest to the cook – such as bunches of dried herbs, bouquet garni, and natural spices. These add fragrance as well as visual interest.

THE NEEDLEPERSON'S WREATH

In our final decoration, we have included a number of items of use to the person interested in all aspects of needlecrafts. The aim of this design was to decorate only part of the wicker ring, leaving as much as half of it exposed. Instead of winding it with ribbon to give colour and detail, we have applied a yellow tape measure threaded into the decoration and forming a lightly flourished bow.

The many useful small-scale materials for the sewer or knitter make it easy to include a wide range of shapes, colours and textures that can be attractively arranged. Our example includes a large ball of wool, a zipper, a handy container of dressmaking pins with coloured tips, various colours of sewing and embroidery threads, knitting needles and a crochet hook. These individual elements are fixed in place using pieces of wire or strong thread.

Alternative ideas
The basic principle of the decorated wreaths can be interpreted in all sorts of ways. If, for example, you want a birthday gift for a sporting type, you may not wish to go to the expense of including a major item such as a tennis or squash racket, but there are other smaller things that the recipient will enjoy, such as wristlets or head bands, glucose sweets for energy, and shower-gel or soap for after-match use. If you wish to create a more general design not associated with a particular pastime, you could use any number of delightful bathroom items – soaps, tiny bottles of fragrant oils, sponges, brushes and so on – that would add up to a wonderful gift for an individual.

EDIBLE GIFTS

The items that we have selected as gifts to be eaten and enjoyed have a special touch in that they are that bit more exotic and decorative in themselves than equivalent day-to-day foods, but the real secret of creating a truly delightful edible gift lies in the final presentation. It is important to select attractive containers, like our fruit jars and elegant vinegar bottles, and to add thoughtful personal touches such as the ribbon decorations

and pretty hand-written labels.

HERB VINEGAR

For this, you can use red, white or even cider vinegar. You will also need about 2oz (60g) herbs, lightly crushed in order to release the flavour. You can also add other spices, such as cloves or crushed garlic. The bottle that you use in making the vinegar must be heatproof, but for a more attractive presentation the vinegar can later be siphoned off into a different container.

Put the crushed herbs and spices into the bottle. Top up with vinegar that has just been brought to the boil. Heating the vinegar helps to release the flavours of the crushed herbs. Cap the bottle and leave the herbs in the vinegar for at least two weeks. Store it in a cool, dark place. If you transfer the herb vinegar to another container after this time, include some fresh, uncrushed herbs to give additional colour and texture to the presentation.

Herb-flavoured vinegars are particularly delicious used in butter sauces and salad dressings, or as a base for marinades. The herbs can be selected to complement particular meats or fish – for example, tarragon for chicken dishes and rosemary for lamb.

FRUIT VINEGAR

To make about 2 pints (1.2 litres/5 cups) of fruit vinegar you require 1-1¼ pints (600-750ml/2½-3 cups) white vinegar and 1lb (450g) soft, ripe fruit, such as raspberries or strawberries. Soak the fruit in the vinegar in a sterilized jar or bottle. Seal the container and leave it in a cool place for several weeks, shaking it gently on occasion to make the flavours develop and permeate through all the vinegar.

When the flavours have developed to taste, strain the vinegar through muslin (or through a coffee filter). Press the berries to extract as much flavour as possible. If you wish, add about 2oz (50g) sugar to the vinegar and simmer for about 10 minutes to soften the sharpness of the fruit flavour. Strain the vinegar into sterilized bottles and store in a cool place. A further sediment may form, which is quite harmless but you can strain it off if you wish.

To make lemon pear vinegar, use one pear cut into quarters and a half-lemon cut into wedges, and follow the procedure as above.

Fruit vinegars are delicious in marinades for fish or meat. Lemon pear vinegar is particularly wonderful with fish. They can also be used for making fruit-flavoured mayonnaise or dips for

crudités, and give added freshness to salad dressings.

PEACHES AND APRICOTS IN BRANDY

8 large, ripe peaches
12 apricots
2½lb (1.3kg)/5 cups sugar
1pt (600ml)/2½ cups brandy
water

Half-fill a large saucepan with water and bring to the boil. Immerse the peaches in the water and poach for about 4 minutes. Poach the apricots for a couple of minutes. Drain the fruits and skin, leaving the fruits whole.

Make a syrup by placing 8oz (250g)/1 cup sugar in a saucepan with 1pt (600ml)/2½ cups water. Stir over a gentle heat until the sugar dissolves, bring to the boil, and boil for 2 minutes. Add the skinned fruit and simmer for 1 minute. Remove the fruit, drain and cool.

Measure 1pt (600ml)/2½ cups of the syrup into a saucepan. Add the remaining sugar and heat gently, stirring until the sugar dissolves. Using a pastry brush dipped in cold water, wash down any sugar crystals that may have formed on the side of the pan to prevent the syrup from crystallizing. Bring to the boil and boil steadily for 2 minutes until the sugar reaches 216°F (102°C) on a sugar thermometer. Plunge the base of the pan immediately into cold water to prevent any further cooking. Allow to cool. Pack the fruit in a large glass storage jar. Pour equal quantities of syrup and brandy over the fruit to cover them. Seal and store in a cool, dry place for up to 6 months.

BOUQUET GARNI

An indispensible and delicious addition to the cook's food stores, bouquet garni are easy to make using fresh, dried or even pre-packaged herbs. The herbs always included in traditional bouquet garni are thyme, parsley and a bay leaf. Additional herbs suitable for particular dishes include basil, sage, garlic and allspice berries.

The bouquet garni is wrapped in a square of muslin and tied with string. However, if you are using fresh herbs you can tie them together in small bunches and arrange them in a pretty box as an alternative presentation for the gift.

MULLED WINE SACHETS

The idea of these fragrant sachets for flavouring mulled wine is the same as that for bouquet garni, but using ingredients such as cinnamon sticks, whole cloves, allspice berries and dried orange peel. The ingredients are wrapped in muslin and tied.

GOOD THINGS IN SMALL PACKAGES

Gift bags and boxes are the perfect containers for home-made delicacies such as marshmallows, treacle toffee and chocolate-dipped strawberries shown here. Beautiful packaging puts the finishing touch to a thoughtfully prepared gift and you don't have to spend a fortune on it. In the following pages we explain how to make attractive three-dimensional packaging, like the gift boxes pictured below. Recipes for a variety of delicious sweetmeats can also be found on pages 92 and 93.

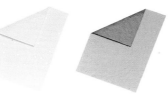

GIFT WRAPPINGS

There are so many wonderful designs for gift-wrap papers and decorative accessories that choosing the wrappings can be as much pleasure as selecting or making the actual gift. Our ideas show how you can use gift papers (opposite) and everyday paper materials in new and inventive ways. Attractive two-way papers (above) are easily made by sticking tissue or even newspaper pages to coloured paper. Combining colours, patterns and textures is a sure way to achieve an unusual presentation.

GIFT PACKS AND BOXES

Solid silver shapes make a highly elegant effect (above), but each of our gift boxes is very simply made by folding up one piece of textured paper in the correct manner to achieve the crisp three-dimensional shape. Simple folds are also the secret of the attractive envelope-style gift packs (left), made with layers of paper in the striking combination of orange, black and gold. All of these packages are highly suited to small, personal gifts for birthday or anniversary celebrations, and certainly add to the sense of a special occasion that merits special attention.

INDIVIDUAL GREETINGS

An envelope with newsprint lining makes a bold effect, matched by a collaged card using headline type to carry your personally selected message of greeting.

GIFT PACKAGING

When you have taken time and trouble to make a personalized gift or to shop for something special, it is appropriate to make a little additional effort to present it beautifully packaged. Here we show you several simple but stunning ideas for gift packaging, using shining silver to create perfect geometric containers and gold as a lining for envelope-style packages. Of course, much of the pleasure of packaging can result from combining colours and textures to produce something beautiful and unusual, a unique expression of your own style and taste. You can choose from the great range of coloured papers and cards, from pretty floral prints to bold abstract patterns, from brightly coloured plain papers to glittering metallic foils. You can even use everyday materials to make fresh, surprising gift wrappings. There is no limit to the number of ways you can create special effects very simply using readily available, inexpensive materials, and there is no need to limit yourself to paper wrappings. There is no reason why a gift should not be wrapped in fabric, or perhaps more than one fabric. You can add ribbons or pompom bows or festive ornaments. We recommend that you also look at our section on decorating with stencil patterns (pages 122-124), which may inspire you with other ideas for attractive and individual forms of presentation.

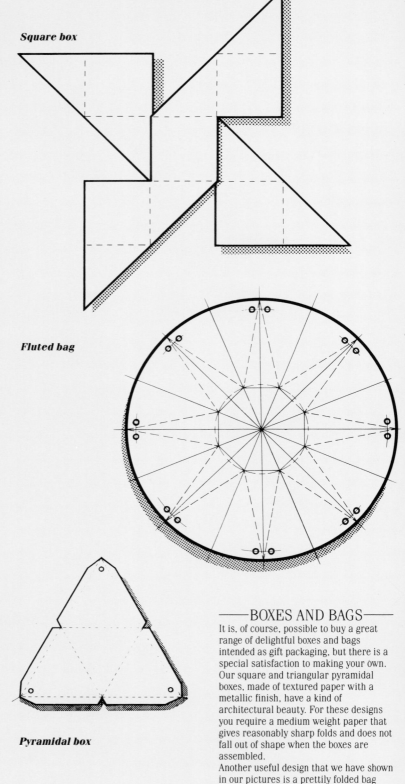

Square box

Fluted bag

Pyramidal box

BOXES AND BAGS

It is, of course, possible to buy a great range of delightful boxes and bags intended as gift packaging, but there is a special satisfaction to making your own. Our square and triangular pyramidal boxes, made of textured paper with a metallic finish, have a kind of architectural beauty. For these designs you require a medium weight paper that gives reasonably sharp folds and does not fall out of shape when the boxes are assembled.

Another useful design that we have shown in our pictures is a prettily folded bag

88

with a flat base and fluted sides, based on a circle of paper. It may take a little effort to get these three-dimensional packages right if it is your first attempt, but once you have understood the simple principles of folding and securing the shapes, you will find it easy to produce very beautiful results quite quickly.

—ENVELOPE-STYLE GIFT— PACKS

Simple ways of folding combined layers of paper produce highly special and unusual packaging for small gifts such as jewellery, handkerchiefs or a fine scarf – anything that can be packaged flatly without damage. We have adapted three ideas for folded packages; a basic envelope, made from three layers of paper, with the edges unsealed but secured with gold cord; a slip-in pack made from two strips of coloured paper folded together and interlocked; and a flat-pack wallet with ribbon tie. Using layers of different-coloured papers turns these simple items into quite substantial and highly decorative packaging. You can also use the envelope to contain a matching invitation or gift card, as shown in the Libra birthday on pages 42-45.

Flat-pack gift wallet

This is similar to the envelope in principle but the folds are more complex, producing a beautiful layered effect that gradually unfolds. Two coloured paper squares folded back to back are all you need, and a length of ribbon to make the ties.

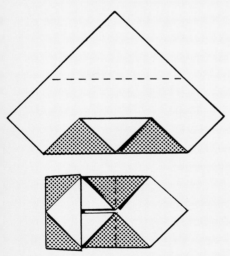

Slip-in pack

For this you need two strips of coloured paper. The method of constructing the pack is based on three folds and the proportions of length to width of the paper strips work on a basis of approximately seven to one.

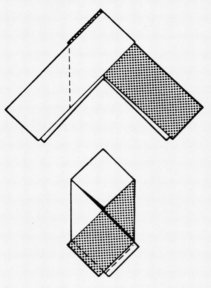

—MAKING WRAPPINGS — AND CARDS

Our pictures show how even humble newsprint can be used in inventive ways to contribute bold visual texture to gift wrappings and cards. While you may enjoy using purpose-made decorative papers for your wrappings, there is also a lot of fun to be had from trying out everyday materials. Brown paper of the type used for ordinary packages, for example, gains a delightful texture when scrunched up tightly and then opened out and ironed over. The tracery of creases and folds can be decorated by spraying with colour or applying stencil motifs. You can use the layered approach shown in our envelope-style packages to create interesting effects of colour and texture for your wrappings and cards using ordinary, everyday printed materials. It may be possible to vary the weights and textures of the papers by including tissue or cellophane, for example, recycled from the wrappings of your own gifts or purchases.

Newspaper and magazine pages provide bold and attractive typography that can be cut out and reassembled to create your personal greeting on a birthday card or party invitation. Colour illustrations or photographs may contribute unusual motifs and textures that could also be included in collaged designs.

MARSHMALLOWS

2tbsp (30ml) icing sugar
2tbsp (30ml) cornflour
1lb (450g)/2 cups granulated sugar
1½ tbsp (25ml) liquid glucose
½pt (300ml)/1¼ cups water
3tbsp (45ml) rose water
1oz (25g) gelatin powder
red food colour
2 egg whites

Sift a little icing sugar and cornflour together and use it to coat the sides of an oiled shallow tin. Shake out any excess. Place the granulated sugar, glucose and 7 fl oz (200ml) of the water in a heavy-based pan. Stir over gentle heat until the sugar dissolves. Using a brush dipped in water, brush down any sugar crystals from the sides of the pan. Bring to the boil and boil without stirring until the temperature reaches 260°F (127°C) on a sugar thermometer.
Place the remaining water and the rose water in a bowl. Sprinkle the gelatin over the liquid. Leave to soften for a couple of minutes, then place the bowl over a pan of hot water and stir until the gelatin has dissolved. Add the colouring, then stir the liquid glucose into the syrup. Remove the pan from the heat immediately. Pour the syrup in a thin stream onto the egg whites, beating constantly. Beat for 3 minutes or until thickened. Pour the mixture into the prepared tin and leave to set for at least four hours.
Ease the mixture away from the sides of the tin with a greased knife, then gradually ease it away from the base. Sift the remaining icing sugar and cornflour onto a baking tray and turn the slab of marshmallow onto it. Turn over and coat on the other side. Cut into 1in (2.5cm) squares and store in an airtight, paper-lined container for up to 10 days. Alternatively, the marshmallow can be cut into heart shapes using a biscuit cutter first dipped in hot water to prevent sticking.

TREACLE TOFFEE

4oz (125g)/½ cup butter
12oz (350g)/½ cup demerara sugar
12oz (350g) black treacle

Melt the butter over gentle heat, then stir in the sugar and the treacle. Place a warmed sugar thermometer into the toffee and cook over a moderately low heat, stirring frequently, until the temperature reaches 266°F (130°C), or the light crack stage.
Immediately plunge the base of the pan into a bowl of cold water to prevent further cooking. Pour the toffee into a greased 8in (20cm) square tin. As the toffee begins to set, cut it into 1in (2.5cm) squares.
Store the pieces in an airtight tin, individually wrapped in greased paper, if you wish.

89

CHAPTER 6

ROMANTIC THEMES

There is one simple way to introduce romance into your party foods and decorations – make everything heart-shaped and your loved one cannot fail to understand your message. For beautiful edible Valentines, quite appropriate for special celebrations at any time of year, we have produced a variety of ideas for delicious heart-shaped cakes and sweetmeats, perfectly presented. Thoughtful preparation and presentation are among the most important aspects of creating a romantic mood. Use the most sumptuous ingredients and give equal attention to those decorative extras that illustrate the truly personal touch.

There are many themes and moods that have romantic associations and these can be interpreted in many ways. As a contrast to the items on these pages that are highly ornamental but also completely edible, we have created a delightful sculpture of non-edible materials that forms the decoration on a cake specially designed for the music lover (see page 44). This makes a wonderful centrepiece, but the idea is that once the party is over you can convert the assemblage into a permanent decoration, in the form of a garland to hang on the wall.

ROMANTIC TREATS

Small, sweet delicacies beautifully presented are a perfect contribution to the romantic birthday celebration or Valentine's Day party. The picture shows (clockwise from centre) sweet biscuits shaped with a heart-shaped cutter and wrapped in metallic foil, finger-sized pieces of delicious chocolate crunch cake, heart-shaped pieces of Greek halva with a softly marbled texture, and cubes of citrus-flavoured Turkish delight.

RASPBERRY HEART

Masses of fresh fruit laced around with tiny white gypsophila flowers make a sumptuous centrepiece for the romantic birthday. Beneath the rich layer of fruit is a heart-shaped cake layered with raspberry conserve and mascarpone (a creamy, sweet cheese) and moistened with dessert wine. The romantic appreciates the finest ingredients and beautiful presentation. Flowers are always an essential symbol of true romance and can be used to decorate individual dishes, the party table and the room.

GOLDEN HEART

Accompanied by a single red rose, the golden heart could be a beautiful gift for the romantic, but it is actually a delicious and unusual cake, completely edible including the gold covering. This is made of the finest gold leaf, an extravagant gesture but one which produces a glittering effect that cannot be matched by any other form of cake decoration. The cake is made in a heart-shaped mould (as shown left), which is first lined with marzipan, than packed with a chocolate truffle mixture that needs no baking. When the cake is turned out of the mould the gold leaf is applied in individual fine sheets until the surface is completely covered. All the decorative detail of the mould is picked up by the marzipan layer and is enhanced by the reflectiveness of the gold leaf.

91

THE ROMANTIC

Producing a stunning birthday celebration for the true romantic is straightforward and easy. It simply depends on using the most sumptuous and beautiful ingredients presented in ways that appeal to the eye and the palate. We have created a range of delicious cakes and sweetmeats that cannot fail to delight. To these you can add fine wines, flowers and thoughtful decoration to make the romantic birthday an occasion to remember. The centrepiece of the celebration is a lavish raspberry cake in the shape of a heart, full of sweet tastes and scents. As a complement, we have created a small heart-shaped cake filled with rich chocolate truffle mixture and covered with real gold leaf – an eye-catching and irresistible addition to the party table. Our final presentation consists of small sweetmeats, cake slices and biscuits beautifully arranged on fine china, contributing a variety of tastes and textures to the feast. Using heart-shaped cutters to cut biscuits or sweets is a very apt way of continuing the romantic theme and metallic wrappings add an extra touch of sparkle.

FOR THE RASPBERRY HEART

heart-shaped cake
dessert wine
raspberry conserve
mascarpone (or soft cream cheese)
fresh raspberries

RASPBERRY HEART

We suggest that for this you use a fairly plain cake and make the fillings extremely rich and generous. Ideally, the cake would be baked in a heart-shaped tin, but it can equally be made in a round tin and carved to a heart shape when it has been layered with fillings and allowed to sit for a while.

We split our cake into layers and moistened them with sweet dessert wine. One layer was then filled with raspberry conserve, a second with mascarpone, an Italian product that is like a slightly sweetened cream cheese. You can, of course, choose the fillings to your own taste, but we recommend using a rich fruit conserve rather than a sweet jam for the fruit layer, even though a conserve may be a little more expensive. It adds flavour and freshness, and is also used as an effective "adhesive" layer for the raspberries on top of the cake.

Choose only the firmest and finest fruit for the topping. Even out of season, you may be able to find fresh imported fruit and the best quality really does improve the taste and texture of the cake.

After shaping the cake, the top was spread with conserve and the fresh raspberries loaded on to the surface, preserving the shape of the heart. We put the cake on the prettiest plate we could find and, as a finishing touch, added small bunches of delicate white gypsophila forming a lacy frill around the edge of the cake.

FOR THE GOLDEN HEART

heart-shaped mould
1lb (450g) marzipan
chocolate truffle mix
24-carat gold leaf, about 6 sheets

GOLDEN HEART

A heart-shaped mould forms the attractive contour of this cake, which we have enhanced by covering it with real gold leaf. This may seem a relatively expensive item for cake decoration, but it certainly creates something extra special and 24-carat gold leaf is perfectly edible.

The leaf is sold in small booklets containing a number of individual sheets and it is obtainable from artists' suppliers.

The mould used here was 6in (15cm) across. To cover a cake of this size you will need about five or six sheets of gold leaf. It needs to be handled with care and patience as the sheets are very fine and will easily tear if you apply too much pressure when moulding them onto the cake. You need to work in a draught-free room, as any breath of air can carry away the lightweight leaf.

The cake is made by lining a mould with marzipan and filling it with chocolate truffle mixture. If you do not wish to use a gold covering, you can create a very decorative effect by colouring the marzipan with a marbled texture, that is, not working the colour right through it, before you use it to line the mould. Alternatively, you can simply ice the cake with a smooth white layer of fondant icing and use flowers and ribbons to add colour to the presentation.

1 On a work surface lightly dusted with cornflour, roll out 1lb (450g) marzipan into a sheet about $1/4$in (6mm) thick.

2 Feed the marzipan sheet into the mould and lightly press it into the detail. Trim the marzipan around the top of the mould.

3 Fill the lined mould with chocolate truffle mixture (our recipe needs no cooking). Pack the mixture down firmly to leave no gaps within the mould.

4 Invert the mould on a plate or cake board and tap it on the work surface to release the cake from the mould and allow it to drop out onto the plate or board.

5 Brush the surface of the marzipan with a little egg white to make an adhesive base for the gold leaf. Using a sable hair paintbrush, lift a sheet of gold leaf and lay it gently on the cake. Dab the gold very gently to pick up all the moulded detail on the surface.

6 Continue to build up the gold covering, applying one leaf at a time. When it is complete, trim the excess gold around the base of the cake.

CHOCOLATE TRUFFLE CAKE (unbaked)

4oz (125g) dark chocolate
2oz (60g)/¼ cup butter
2 egg yolks
8oz (250g)/about 3 cups cake crumbs
2oz (60g) cocoa powder (optional)
2 tbsp (30ml) brandy (optional)

(You may need to double or treble these quantities to produce a larger batch of the mixture depending on the size of your mould.)
Break the chocolate into pieces and put it in a bowl with the butter.
Place the bowl over a pan of gently boiling water and leave the chocolate to melt, turning it once or twice. Remove the bowl from the pan and stir in the egg yolks, cocoa powder (optional, but it does give depth to the chocolate flavour), cake crumbs and brandy. Mix thoroughly.
Leave for a couple of hours to allow the mixture to absorb the liquid. For use it should be firm to the touch, capable of being rolled into balls as for petit fours.
Note: For the cake crumbs, madeira cake is best for this recipe but you can use other kinds that may also change the flavour; for example, ginger cake.

───ROMANTIC TREATS───

Plenty of small and delicious things complete the romantic mood of this celebration. You can, of course, serve any kind of sweetmeats, tiny biscuits or cakes, and we have included here a few recipes for the items shown in our picture.

A simple and appropriate way to give a special meaning to these items is to cut out the sweetmeats or biscuits with a heart-shaped cutter. We have used one of these to shape the attractively marbled pieces of the exquisite Greek delight, halva. You could cut marshmallows, biscuits or sweet pastry in the same way, depending on your own tastes or those of your guests.

The idea represented in the golden heart cake can be reworked on this smaller scale by wrapping heart-shaped sweetmeats in thin metallic foil, as in our plateful of blue hearts. Foils are available from good cookware shops. They are almost as fragile as gold leaf and add beautiful touches of glitter to the party food, but they are quite inexpensive.

HALVA

10oz (300g)/1¼ cups granulated sugar
2 egg whites, beaten stiff
4oz (125g)/½ cup honey (warmed)
5oz (150g)/1 cup ground almonds

Beat the sugar into the egg whites and continue to beat until the sugar has dissolved. Add the honey and put the mixing bowl over a pan of hot water on gentle heat. Cook for 25 minutes, stirring constantly. When the mixture has thickened to a paste, stir in the almonds. Use a wet palette knife to spread the mixture in a Swiss roll tin lined with baking parchment. Leave to set in a cool place for a day or two. Cut the halva to shape as required.

TURKISH DELIGHT

strained juice and thinly pared rind of 1 lemon
strained juice and thinly pared rind of 1 orange
1lb (450g) lump sugar
½pt (300ml)/1¼ cups water
1oz (30g) powdered gelatin
2 tbsp icing sugar
1 tbsp cornflour

Dissolve the lump sugar in half the water over a medium heat. Add the strips of lemon and orange rind and the juices. Bring the mixture to the boil and simmer for 15 minutes.
Soften the gelatin by soaking it in the rest of the water for 5 minutes. Add the gelatin to the sugar syrup and boil, stirring well, for 20 minutes. Strain the mixture into a wet shallow tin and leave for 24 hours to set. Cut into cubes. Sieve the icing sugar and cornflour and roll the pieces of Turkish delight in the mixture. Stack the pieces in boxes with more icing sugar and cornflour mixture in between them.
Different flavours can be made by leaving out the orange and adding rose water or crème de menthe to taste. Food colours can also be added, to give the Turkish delight a pink tinge, for example.

CHOCOLATE CRUNCH CAKE

6oz (180g) dark chocolate
4oz (125g)/½ cup butter
14oz (420g)/1¾ cups condensed milk
10oz (300g) digestive biscuits, roughly broken
2oz (60g) raisins
4oz (125g) glacé cherries (halved)

Put the chocolate, butter and condensed milk into a heavy-based saucepan. Heat gently until melted, stirring occasionally. Add the broken biscuits, raisins and cherries and stir well.
Line an 8in (20cm) round cake tin with kitchen foil. Press the mixture into the tin and chill until firm. Remove from the tin and foil. Dust with sifted cocoa powder. Cut into slices and serve.

THE MUSIC LOVER

This beautiful decoration is created from readily acquired basic materials and is assembled on a simple ring-shaped cake decorated with two colours of marzipan. The main part of the decoration consists of photocopies of sheet music rolled into cones, and looped and bunched ribbons of varying colours and widths. These are attached to a crescent-shaped cardboard backing. Miniature ornamental musical instruments are finally put in place and the whole assembly is mounted on the cake. To give an even more lavish effect to the presentation, the cake is placed on fanned-out flat music sheets. The rich colours and textures are evocative of romantic musical themes and the beauty of the polished and detailed instruments on which they are played.

Assembling the decoration *Roll copies of music sheets into cone shapes.*

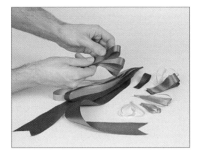

Make folded and looped bunches of varying widths and colours of ribbon.

For the garland, cut out a poem and 'age' the edges by colouring and curling them.

Attach the music sheets and ribbons to a cardboard backing of suitable shape.

MUSICAL GARLAND

The hanging garland is created from exactly the same decoration as that used for the cake. After the cake has been cut and eaten, the musical ornaments with their rich background of ribbons and music sheets are mounted on a wreath of fine twigs and branches sprayed with gold. In this way, what might have been a temporary decoration for a birthday cake becomes a delightful permanent decoration giving mood and atmosphere to the room. For display, the garland has here been bound around with wide ribbon of a warm, glossy red-brown and a decorative bow attaches it to the light fitting.

THE MUSIC LOVER

This elaborate and romantic design evolved from the idea of creating an edible centrepiece for a celebration, in the form of the cake, but with non-edible decoration that could be transformed into a permanent display, as a garland to hang on the wall. The various items are assembled on a stiff cardboard backing cut to a rough crescent shape that follows the curve of the cake. The entire decoration is simply removed in one piece when it comes time to cut the cake and, when the party is over, it is easily attached to a circular wreath to form the hanging garland.

The theme of the music lover sets the colour scheme of rich browns and oranges, reflecting the beautiful varnished and polished woods of which musical instruments may be made, and the lavish ribbon decorations are an essentially romantic touch. Fanned and rolled music sheets (actually photocopies of a single sheet of music) continue the theme, adding the contrast of black and white and the textural interest of the musical notation.

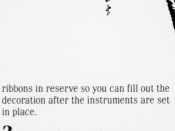

FOR THE MUSIC LOVER CAKE
stiff cardboard
sheet music (photocopies)
ribbons
miniature musical instruments
gold paint
12in (30cm) ring-shaped cake
2lb (900g) marzipan
food colours: orange, brown

THE CAKE

Making the decoration

For this design you need a piece of stiff cardboard, several copies of a sheet of music, ribbons of various widths and colours, and ornamental musical instruments. The ones that we used were two small Christmas tree ornaments and a miniature piece that came from a gift shop. These have some of the beauty of the originals that they represent, in their rich colours and fine detail.

If you cannot find suitable miniatures or replicas in a gift or toy store, you might use inexpensive real instruments, such as penny whistles, or if you are using the decoration for a child's birthday party, you could include a recorder that would actually be the birthday gift, incorporated in the cake decoration. Alternatively, good quality colour photographs cut from magazines can be mounted on card and inserted in the decoration. These lack the depth of the model instruments but carefully selected and presented, photographs could prove just as effective. An attractive touch that gives character to the design is to give the music sheets the impression of aged paper, either by having them photocopied on cream or parchment paper, or by colouring them lightly at the edges. They also look very decorative if you spray the edges with a little gold paint before rolling the sheets.

1 Cut the cardboard backing to a crescent shape suited to the size of the cake. Our example is about 8in (20cm) long and 3in (8cm) wide. Roll the music sheets into cone shapes and staple or glue them to the cardboard backing. Concentrate them at the top and bottom of the piece but fan them out into an attractive shape.

2 Fold the ribbons into looped bunches and use staples or adhesive to attach them to the card. Arrange the ribbon loops so that the different widths and colours create an interesting overall form to the design incorporating variations of shape, colour and texture. Keep a few ribbons in reserve so you can fill out the decoration after the instruments are set in place.

3 Arrange the musical instruments among the ribbons. How you attach them depends on whether you wish to be able to remove them later. They can be fixed in place with adhesive or tied on with fine wire or strong thread. Add further ribbons if there are any gaps in the design.

4 To complete the decoration, attach longer loops of ribbon hanging down from the instruments and two long, wide trailing pieces cut into V-shapes at the ends.

Decorating the cake

Our example is a 12in (30cm) round cake with the centre cut out, using a saucer as a guide, to create the ring shape. The edges were trimmed off to create a more rounded finish. Alternatively, you can cook the cake initially in a ring mould. The decoration made is by colouring marzipan and making this the finishing layer. The marzipan is simply arranged in alternating bands of colour around the ring.

1 Cover the cake with a thin layer of sieved apricot jam. Take 2lb (900g) marzipan, divide it in two and colour the halves separately with the required colours.

2 Roll out the marzipan into large sheets. From each colour, cut strips about 2-2½in (5-6cm) wide and long enough to fit over the cake ring from the outer edge to the inner. Because the inner circumference of the cake is considerably smaller than the outer, you will need to taper the strips slightly down the length so that they will fit to the inner ring.

3 Lay the marzipan strips over the cake in alternating bands of colour. Trim the strips as necessary to fit them to each other and to the shape of the cake. It is not necessary to look for geometric precision in creating the colour bands. Simply position and trim them by eye to create a fairly even effect.

4 Allow the marzipan to dry completely before placing the decoration in position on the cake.

THE GARLAND

The basic wreath on which the decoration is displayed as a hanging garland can be bought or made (see also pages 82 and 84).

Our example is a wreath about 14in (35cm) in diameter made of entwined, slender branches. This was sprayed with gold paint and allowed to dry.

To attach the decoration to the garland, simply position the cardboard backing on the wreath and use fine wire (or strong thread) to bind it unobtrusively to the wreath. Wind a piece of wide ribbon around the garland and tie the ends into a bow that can be used to hang up the finished garland.

As an additional decoration adding to the mood of the piece, we attached a small sheet of poetry to the side of the garland opposite the musical decoration. We had a Shakespearean sonnet photocopied on paper the same colour as that used for the music sheets and trimmed it with an irregular line around the edges to give an aged effect. To add to the appearance of an old document, we singed the edges of the paper lightly by running a match flame below them.

If you do this, bear in mind the dangers of working with a naked flame. The idea is not to set light to the paper but simply to darken it slightly, giving it additional colour and texture. An alternative way to achieve this effect is to spray the irregularly cut edges with gold paint and curl the corners gently by drawing them over a knife or scissor blade.

CHAPTER 7

GOOD ENOUGH TO EAT

When giving a party, you naturally take some trouble to present the food in attractive ways, but perhaps you don't have an infinite supply of beautiful serving dishes for all the sumptuous items that you have made. We can solve this problem by pointing out how beautiful containers can be made wholly from natural and edible materials, in many cases from the same source that supplies your party foods. The skins and outer layers of many fruits and vegetables make excellent natural containers, so rather than discard them you can put them to decorative use. We have suggested a number of ways in which they can be creatively used for colourful and delicious presentation of party dishes.

We have also created a delightful lacy spaghetti bowl that you will find perfect for serving delicate and tasty savouries. Following on from this theme, we have investigated the potential of ice bowls as serving dishes. Our designs use colour to enhance the eye-catching effect of the glistening ice.

98

PEPPER BOATS

Glistening, colourful peppers make ideal containers for a savoury dip accompanying crisp crudités. When you choose which dips to serve, consider the colours as well as the flavours you wish to present. Cut and fill the peppers only minutes before serving, so that the skins do not have time to lose their firmness.

SPAGHETTI BOWL

The charming lacy texture and natural golden colour of the deep-fried spaghetti bowl makes a particularly good complement to the rich colours of Chinese food. Here the bowl contains glistening spare ribs accompanied by lightly blanched snow peas.

ORANGES AND MELONS

The bright yellow swan, made from a honeydew melon, is an elegant natural container for fresh strawberries. The lotus blossom carved from an orange encloses a lemon sorbet topped with jewel-like pomegranate seeds. In the second orange container, lychees and ice-cream are concealed beneath a golden meringue topping.

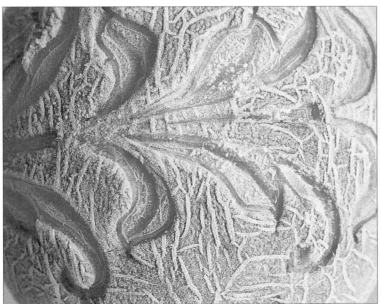

CARVED OGEN MELONS

The stencil design, taken from a Victorian pattern book, was carved, not too deeply, using special V-tools (top right), but ordinary kitchen implements will do. The swirling leaves show finely against the heavy white bloom on the frozen melon skin (above). A decoratively cut Ogen melon, with seeds removed but the flesh left inside, makes a delicious individual dessert when filled with raspberry purée (right).

99

EDIBLE CONTAINERS

Nature not only provides us with a wealth of exquisite and delicious fruits and vegetables, but is clever enough to pack many of them in the most beautiful skins. Too little is made of the beauty of the exterior, which is often stripped away or cut off and discarded. We have illustrated some inventive ways in which fruits and vegetables can be used as containers, adding to the look, and sometimes also the smell and taste, of the other foods served in them. With certain kinds of fruit, you can simply use the decorative outer layers as the container for the scooped-out flesh, creating a fresh, different presentation without the need for extra ingredients, but we have also suggested ideas for combining delicious tastes and textures, for example, by adding sorbet, purée or meringue to the fruit.

Another variation on the theme of edible containers is represented by the crisp, delicate spaghetti bowl, intricate in appearance but surprisingly easy to make. If you like the idea of creating the container yourself rather than using a natural receptacle, turn to the ideas for the Taurean birthday, on pages 22-25, where you will find a golden dough basket that makes a perfect container for light cheeses, biscuits and fruits.

─PEPPER SAUCE-BOATS─

Medium-sized vegetables and fruits with firm skins make excellent individual containers. Attractive boats to hold savoury sauces or dips are easily made from colourful peppers. Take two large and perfect peppers, one red and one green, and polish the skins to a beautifully sleek, waxy finish. Simply cut the peppers in half, or carve out a section from the top to form a decorative shape. Then scoop out the seeds, and fill the pepper with the sauce or dip, with an eye to its colour as a complement or contrast to the colour of the pepper.

It is best not to prepare peppers in this way too far in advance of serving, as although they are quite firm and crisp to begin with, they do start to wilt quite quickly.

──SPAGHETTI BOWL──

Constructing the spaghetti bowl is quite time-consuming, but the final effect is stunning. You will need two colanders or sieves that will sit inside a deep-fat fryer or a large pan that you can actually fill with hot oil.

1 Boil some hot water and simmer your spaghetti until it is bendable and can be handled. When it has the right texture, drain the spaghetti and run it under cold water.

2 Working quickly, take five or six strands of spaghetti and fold them in half. Arrange them in your colander or sieve with the loose ends at the bottom and the looped ends hanging slightly over the top edge.

3 Work in the same way so that you have groups of looped strands all around the edge of the colander or sieve. If you have spare strands of spaghetti left over, drape them around the bottom and slightly up the sides, to give extra strength to the base of the spaghetti bowl.

4 Heat the oil in a deep-fryer or large pan. Place your second colander or sieve over the spaghetti in the first one and lower the whole thing into the oil. Arrange some sort of handle to secure the two colanders or sieves so that you can easily and safely lower them into the oil and remove them.

5 Allow about 5 or 10 minutes in fairly hot oil for the spaghetti to cook and turn golden. When it has reached the colour that you like, remove it and allow it to drain. Don't touch it too quickly; wait until it has lost some of its heat.

6 Remove the top colander or sieve and gently prise the spaghetti away from the lower one. It may have stuck slightly, in which case just pull it gently but persistently. Allow the bowl to stand on kitchen paper for a while, to drain the excess oil, before you use it to serve food.

MELON-RIND SWAN

A melon rind carved in the shape of a swan is a graceful container and quite easy to make. You can either chop the flesh of the melon and return it to the carved rind container or, if the swan is used to hold something else, you can put the melon flesh into fresh fruit drinks or desserts.

1 Mark out the shape of the swan on the melon, using a food-colour pen.

2 Using a sharp kitchen knife, cut through the skin into the flesh of the melon, following the lines you have drawn.

3 Take hold of the section of melon above the carving and ease it away from the lower piece.

4 Using a spoon or melon-baller scoop out the flesh from inside the two sections of the melon.

LOTUS-FLOWER ORANGE

The orange is very simply carved, but it makes a decorative and neatly sized container. Again, you can use the flesh of the fruit for making a sorbet, fruit salad or fresh juice.

1 Draw the lotus petals on the top half of the orange, using a food-colour pen.

2 Put a sharp knife straight through into the centre of the orange, along each of the lines of the petals. If you do this correctly, it should be possible to pull away the top part in one piece. Save the 'lid' and turn it into the base of the container, as in the picture.

3 The next step is to scoop out the flesh of the orange, which is not as simple as it sounds. Do not simply gouge out the interior or you may tear the skin. Use a small spoon and work slowly and patiently.

Preserving freshness
Once you take the flesh from a fruit, the skin can quickly become limp and your container may collapse. To avoid this, as soon as you have removed the flesh, put the container into the deep freeze. This way it remains rigid until you are ready to fill and serve.

CARVED OGEN MELON

The carved melon looks rather elaborate, but it is simply done by following a stencil pattern. Draw the pattern on the rind and carve out the areas of skin within the shapes. For carving, we used lino-cutting tools, but you could work with a potato peeler or just a sharp knife, cutting in a V-like cross-section. Avoid cutting deeply into the flesh or the juices will escape. You can create an additional level of detail by applying food colour to the exposed areas, enhancing their contrast with the colour and texture of the rind. The Ogen melon has a particularly attractive exterior and its bloom is enhanced by deep freezing, the frosted effect picking out the textural details in pure white. Be careful when you transfer the melon from freezer to table as the heat of your fingers will quickly remove the frosty coating.
While the Ogen melon has a particular decorative value, the technique works just as well with honeydew or water melons. You can even use it on a squash or pumpkin, to make a container for a savoury meal such as a risotto. This makes an attractive style of presentation for vegetarian dishes.

Individual melon containers
Ogen melons are quite small and can be used as containers for sweet sauces, in the same way as the peppers containing savoury dips, or for serving as individual desserts. An idea that takes advantage of both the attractive skin of the melon and the colour and flavour of its flesh is to create decorative melon containers holding fresh fruit purée.
Simply cut into the top of the melon to create a decorative shape, scoop out the seeds from inside and fill the cavity with purée. Raspberry purée is a particularly good choice, its sharpness forming a perfect complement to the sweet flesh of the melon.

101

SALAD BOWLS

A deliciously fresh effect is achieved by freezing chopped and whole salad vegetables into a clear ice bowl (left). They are not all completely trapped within the ice – the brightly coloured pieces seem to emerge from pure glass. Cold tea and orange juice are the surprising ingredients of a bowl with gently striped and merging, natural coloration (above), the perfect vehicle for a light summer salad decorated with fresh flowers.

AZURE BOWL

The rich shades of blue in this antique-effect bowl demand to be matched by equally colourful contents. Scarlet strawberries are the perfect complement. The depth of tone and texture in the bowl are the result of freezing coloured ice cubes into coloured water. The slightly crazed and clouded texture was inspired by the lovely piece of Venetian glass included in this picture.

ICE MOULDS

This glistening fish was simply made by freezing water in a copper mould usually intended for shaping a savoury mousse. This makes an attractive presentation for fresh seafood, either used as a buffet table centrepiece or served as a starter for a dinner party. Virtually any kind of ordinary kitchen mould can be used in this way, so you can select a decorative shape suited to the food you are serving. If you wish to create a more colourful effect than the glassy surface of clear ice, this is easily achieved by adding food colour to the water before you fill the mould.

DECORATING WITH ICE

Most people imagine ice decorations to be rather elaborate creations only used in large-scale or special occasion catering, the result of several chefs working long hours in a walk-in freezer sculpting a vast piece of ice. However, there is no reason why simple but stunning centrepieces cannot be made in an ordinary kitchen using a family-size freezer. Our pictures demonstrate the point with three eye-catching ice bowls and a centrepiece made from a basic kitchen mould.
Ice bowls are by no means uncommon and are often included in books on entertaining, but we feel that they rarely reach their full potential because the decoration is typically restricted to a garland of flowers and leaves trapped around the rim of the bowl, leaving the rest of the shape undecorated. This can produce a very pretty result, but it is only one possibility. In our designs we have concentrated on colour, to show how very different effects are easily created within the same simple shape.
There is an interesting point to note on how the quality of the water that you use can affect the appearance of your design. For our azure bowl, for example, we used ordinary tap water containing food colouring and the slight impurities in the water produced a slight cloudiness in the ice that was perfect for the effect we wanted. For the crudités bowl, we wanted the purest form of ice possible to allow the inset colours to shine out, so we used bottled spring water, which resulted in ice of great clarity and purity.

Basic method

The nice thing about ice bowls is that they are very simple and require the minimum of equipment. You need two bowls of different sizes, so that one will fit inside the other leaving a gap of about 1in (2.5cm) all the way around. The bowls must be able to withstand being put into a freezer – Pyrex is the ideal material.

1 Make up a tray of ice cubes. Put a layer of cubes into the bottom of your large bowl and sit the small bowl on top of the ice.

2 Weight down the small bowl with a kitchen weight or small food can. Fill the gap between the two bowls with iced water and put the whole thing into the freezer. Leave it long enough for the water to solidify completely into ice.

3 To release the ice bowl, pour tepid water into the small bowl and gently move it around until it loosens. This happens quite quickly. Remove the small bowl and dip the base of the large bowl into tepid water for a few seconds, to free the ice bowl completely. You can store the ice bowl in the freezer until you need it.
It is important that you use iced water in the second stage. Even cold water will begin to melt the ice cubes almost immediately. This, coupled with the fact that the freezing process takes a little time to start once the bowls are in the freezer, means that the inner bowl will drop and you will not get a good base layer for the ice bowl.

Alternative method

This is somewhat simpler than the previous method, but can only be used for certain kinds of ice decoration. The inner bowl is allowed to float in water and if you add decoration, such as flowers or vegetable pieces, these too will float and tend to collect around the rim of the ice bowl.

1 Pour some water into the large bowl and float the smaller bowl in it. To centre and hold down the second bowl, apply adhesive tape across the edges of both bowls on either side.

2 Fill up the remaining gap between the two bowls with more water and put the two bowls into the freezer. When the ice bowl has solidified, you can detach it from the original bowls in exactly the same way as for the previous method.

——— AZURE BOWL ———

We decided to use colour because we had never seen an ice bowl made with anything other than plain water, forming clear ice. The beautiful strong blue that we chose was achieved simply by adding food paste colour to the water. The bowl was made by the basic method starting with ice cubes, but we made the cubes from a large batch of very dark blue water and used the rest of the water to top up between the bowls.
The freezing process produced a very pretty effect that we had not really anticipated. As the coloured water froze into the ice cubes, the colour became more darkly concentrated towards the centre of each cube and was offset by a paler tone on the outside. With this discovery, we decided to include these pinpoints of colour throughout the bowl, rather than just at the base, so we added ice cubes to the gap between the sides of the two Pyrex bowls after the smaller one had been set in position on an ice cube base. The remaining blue water was then diluted and poured in.
As an obvious consequence, the cubes around the side of the bowl floated in the water and after freezing we had the wonderful effect of the two-toned ice cubes suspended in the third, paler shade of blue.
The inspiration for this bowl was a piece of Venetian glass with a "distressed" surface. Having achieved the colour difference, we decide to try for the aged, slightly crazed effect. After taking the ice bowl out of the freezer, we quickly rubbed

our warm hands over the surface and this was enough to make cracks appear in the ice. The bowl then went back into the freezer, to freeze in the cracks.

SUMMER SALAD BOWL

Our third example was a delightful mistake. We used cold tea to make the bowl, hoping to get a beautiful clear shade of amber. During the freezing process, both the colour and texture seemed to deteriorate. We decided to discontinue the experiment and we released the ice bowl from its mould and put it into the sink to dissolve.
The bowl was not frozen right through and by chance a small hole in the base allowed the interior liquid to drain out. We were fascinated by this accidental creation of a hollow bowl, and decided to try to fill it with another liquid. The only suitable liquid we had was a carton of chilled orange juice, which we poured in through the hole in the base. Then we put the tea bowl back into its original Pyrex bowl, weighted it down with the smaller one and put it back into the freezer.
Not only was the orange juice an interesting colour contrast with the amber tea, the way the particles of the juice froze also gave it a completely different texture. Pure accident produced a very beautiful and unusual bowl that made an excellent container for a light summer salad.
A simpler striped effect can be achieved using the second method of making an ice bowl. Float the small inner bowl on a base level of coloured water and allow this to freeze. Then pour in a second colour and freeze it, then a third. In this way you can build up a stunning bowl banded with brilliant colours.

VEGETABLE BOWL

This bowl was intended to hold crudités and a savoury dip, but could equally be used for serving salad at a dinner party. It was made by the basic method, using ice cubes, with the addition of radishes, cherry tomatoes, green, red and yellow peppers, baby sweetcorn and florets of broccoli and cauliflower. The vegetables were chosen for their bright colours and interesting shapes.
When putting the layer of ice cubes into the bottom of your first bowl, add a handful of vegetables, then put the smaller bowl on top and weight it down. Before you add the iced water, pack vegetables between the sides of the two bowls, allowing gaps for the ice to form

around them but packing them quite tightly so they cannot float but will form decoration throughout the whole shape of the ice bowl. Add the iced water and freeze the bowl.

Timing

If you intend making an ice bowl, or any kind of iced decoration, it is advisable to start the day before your party. You will be surprised how long it takes for the ice to set really hard. In order to prevent any last-minute problems, leave plenty of time for preparation and if your ice decoration is ready before you need it, simply store it in the freezer.
In case you are anxious about your work disappearing before your guests have time to appreciate the effect, it is worth pointing out that an ice bowl is not going to melt immediately before your eyes. You have about 30-45 minutes before the melting is really appreciable, in which time you can have served, eaten and cleared the course for which the ice bowl was the container.

Ideas for ice

In the picture on the previous page, you can see how simply a beautiful ice decoration can be made simply by freezing water in an ordinary kitchen mould. We have used a fish mould to form a centrepiece for serving seafood. For serving desserts, you might create an ice decoration from an attractive jelly mould. It is easy to change the colour simply by colouring the water if you wish.
Another idea that you can easily carry out is to make an ice tray for serving drinks or fruits. You will need a stainless steel tray about 1in (2.5cm) deep, with a pronounced lip. Begin by pouring in coloured water to a depth of about ½in (1.2cm) and allowing it to freeze. Then scatter some flower petals, dipped in water, over the sheet of ice and put them into the freezer to set in place. To finish, just flood the tray with pure water and allow it to freeze into a clear upper layer. To release the ice tray, simply dip the base of the stainless steel tray in tepid water, very briefly, to allow the ice sheet to come loose from the base.
If you like to serve bottles of liquor very cold, you can freeze the bottle into a jacket of ice. You will need a catering-size tin can that accommodates at least two-thirds of the bottle. Simply fill the gap between the bottle and can with water and allow it to freeze. To release the bottle, hold it by the neck, dip the can into tepid water and pull out the bottle surrounded by its ice jacket. For decorative variations on this theme, you might add herbs or colouring to the water before freezing.

105

CHAPTER 8

A SENSE OF THEATRE

The theatre of disguise is the opening theme of this section, with a range of beautiful party masks decorated in a variety of ways. A masquerade is a wonderful way to add colour and intrigue to a party. Our mask designs are mainly based on readily available materials that with minimal skill can be turned into memorable disguises, and we include one rather more elaborate idea that will appeal to the collector – a Neptune mask of beautiful shells and sea creatures. If you prefer a simpler approach, we have also included ideas for making basic fabric masks that can be prettily decorated to add life and colour to a party.

In the second part of this chapter, we have returned to the theatre for inspiration and have produced a wonderful cake for the opera lover, representing the beautiful, tragic Madame Butterfly. As with the theme of disguise, this cake has a deceptive element because its stunningly decorative finish suggests that it is quite difficult to do – and this is not the case at all. There can be problems in sculpting a human figure from soft materials such as cake and icing, but the design of this particular cake shows how easily those problems can be overcome.

THEME MASKS

All kinds of materials can be put to use for imaginative decoration of a mask. The summer mask (top) is swathed in paper ribbon and decorated with dried flowers. The Neptune mask (centre) gains its highly elaborate and delicate effect from a beautifully varied collection of seashells, sea creatures and pearls. For the Bacchus mask (bottom), artificial leaves and fruits are attractively combined with dried hops.

BEDOUIN MASKS

The quality of mystery and intrigue that masks contribute to a party atmosphere is enhanced in these designs by the fact that the masks themselves are partially disguised, heavily veiled in a sculptural drapery of paper ribbon. The texture of the ribbon contributes much to the character of each mask. The mask faces are covered with torn paper ribbon pieces to give them a strangely expressive appearance. The headdresses are simply created from fanned, looped and draped lengths of the ribbon attached at the back of each mask.

107

MASQUERADE

Decorative masks add a wonderful sense of mystery and intrigue to a party, and are surprisingly easy to make. All of the designs shown on the previous pages are based on plain white full-face masks, readily available from suppliers of novelty goods and party decorations. These can be worn on the face, tied with ribbon or elastic, or you can fix the mask to a length of dowelling and carry it in front of the face. You might prefer to make your own simple half-face masks out of cardboard, in which case the ideas for decoration described here can be easily adapted to the shape. Alternatively, the themes and interpretations that we have chosen can be taken simply as inspiration for your own designs, based on materials that are readily available from local suppliers or, as in the case of the seashells on the Neptune mask, that may be part of a collection of decorative objects that you already own and have not thought of using in this way. You should bear in mind, however, the practical aspects of this type of disguise. If the decoration adds much weight to the mask, it may be tiring or uncomfortable to wear it throughout an evening of partying and dancing and some components may be too delicate to stand prolonged wear, so the design should take account of all this.

BEDOUIN MASKS

In these two designs we have enhanced the mysterious character of the masks by veiling the faces. The veiling is made from paper ribbon, a product that comes in a range of colours and provides a wonderfully sculptured effect. Available from paper goods specialists, artists' suppliers or some florists, the paper ribbon is twisted and bound into a rope-like material when you buy it. When unwound it has a creased and crinkled effect that is very versatile for decorative uses.

In addition to the veiling, the masks themselves are covered with torn pieces of paper ribbon, to create a textured finish to the faces. The pieces are applied using spray adhesive. To attach the veils to the masks, you will need a stronger adhesive or double-sided tape.

1 Cover both masks with spray adhesive. Tear pieces of red paper ribbon of varying sizes and spray the back of each piece with adhesive. This will ensure that any overlapping edges will be stuck down. Place the paper ribbon pieces randomly over the surface of each mask to cover them completely. When complete, trim the paper to the edges of the masks and cut around the eyeholes where any paper overlaps them.

2 For the red-veiled mask, cut three strips of paper ribbon about 7in (17cm) in length and attach them to the top of the mask along the inside edge. Spread them to create the fan shape on top of the mask, as shown.

3 Cut two 14in (35cm) strips of paper ribbon. Fix one piece inside the mask at the top left. Bring the ribbon over the forehead of the mask at an angle and attach it to the inside of the right-hand edge, just above eye level. Attach the second piece at the lower left side of the mask and drape it across the mouth and nose, leaving the eyes uncovered. Fix the other end of this piece to the inside of the right-hand edge of the mask. When arranging both sections of the veil, make use of the creases and folds in the paper ribbon to develop the sculptured effect.

4 For the black-veiled mask, cut five strips of paper ribbon about 14in (35cm) long. Attach three pieces to the top of the mask and secure both ends so that the ribbons form generous loops. Use the remaining two strips of paper ribbon to create the veiling on the face, in the same way as that described for the red veiling.

5 As the finishing touch for both masks, decorate the veils with small stones to give a jewelled effect. We have used flat-backed mirrored glass stones that have a beautiful lustre when they catch the light.

SUMMER MASK

This delicate design again uses paper rope to great effect and is very simple to create. The decoration consists of peach-coloured paper ribbon and peach-pink dried flowerheads. A strong all-purpose adhesive can be used to attach these to the mask.

1 Take a selection of dried flowerheads and stick them first around the outside edges of the mask, then coming forward slightly onto the forehead and cheek. Allow time for the adhesive to dry.

2 Take a 90cm (1m) length of paper ribbon and attach one end to the inside of the mask on the right-hand side, roughly at forehead level. Swathe the paper ribbon around the mask, coming back to the point where it was first attached, and fix the ribbon using a little more adhesive. This step can be repeated to build up the layers of paper ribbon around the face.

3 Cut six pieces of paper ribbon each about 6in (15cm) in length. Attach three pieces to the right-hand side of the mask and fan them out to the side. With the remaining three pieces, twist or roll them loosely into rosebud shapes and stick or staple these in position at the side of the mask, just in front of the paper fan.

BACCHUS MASK

To decorate this mask, we have used artificial grapes and leaves and some clusters of dried hops. If these items are difficult to find, you can substitute available materials that similarly complement the theme. Leaf shapes can easily be made from coloured paper or paper ribbon.

1 Spray or sponge the white mask with green water-based paint to give it a faint green tint around the edges and lightly shadowing the eyes.

2 Build up a cluster of leaves at the top of the mask, sticking them on one by one. Bring two or three leaves down onto the cheek of the mask.

3 Fix the grapes in place using adhesive or staples. To complete the mask, add the clusters of dried hops on either side of the bunch of grapes.

NEPTUNE MASK

This beautiful mask is quite simple to make but rather more time-consuming than the other designs. You will need to have a generous collection of seashells in various sizes, together with tiny seahorses, sponges, a coral fan, strings of pearls and individual pearls. Because these decorations have more weight, you will need quite a strong adhesive cement to fix them in place.

This design can of course be adapted to the materials that you have available for a sea theme, but if you study the photograph you can see that a wide range of shapes and textures is needed to create the elaborate and lavish appearance of the Neptune mask.

1 Position the larger elements of the design first, in this case the coral fan cemented behind the top edge of the mask. When this has dried in place, attach the larger starfish, seashells and sponges spreading out from the forehead of the mask over the coral fan.

2 Stick smaller shells to the mask face, together with seahorses and small sponges. Make an arrangement that enhances the modelling of the mask, decorating the face without completely disguising it.

3 Attach individual pearls randomly over the face, extending onto the coral fan. Arrange strings of pearls to drape from the temples of the mask, where they can be glued or stapled in position.

4 When all the decoration is complete and the adhesive has dried, spray or sponge light touches of ice blue water-based paint over the mask and the coral fan.

Simple fabric masks

If you do not wish to use full-face masks such as the ones on which our designs are based, you can quickly and inexpensively make an alternative type of basic mask that can be decorated in a variety of ways. Simply make a loop of wire, twisting the ends of the wire securely, and cover it with a single layer of gauze or other fine fabric that will enable you to see through the mask when it is held in front of your face. You can either paint on the fabric or attach lightweight decorations such as ribbons, feathers, sequins, glitter dust or diamanté. Tie the twisted ends of the wire loop to a length of dowelling, painted or decorated to match the mask, so that you can hold it in front of your face, and you have an effective, lightweight and highly decorative mask made entirely to your own design.

109

MADAME BUTTERFLY

The beauty and drama of one of the world's best-loved operas is captured in this brilliantly painted, delicate figure. A simple carving process produces the basis of the figure. The elaborate clothing is built up with crisp layers of gelatin icing.

Sculpting the cake Stack two 8in (20cm) and two 6in (15cm) cakes, aligned vertically.

Carve away the front and back of the cakes to shape the body and cape of the figure.

Model the underlying form of the figure, adding marzipan limbs.

Cast a head in gelatin icing using a simple doll's face as the mould.

Position the moulded head on the body, filling any gaps with marzipan.

Build up the layers of clothing section by section using pieces of gelatin icing.

MADAME BUTTERFLY

Anyone with a love of the theatrical cannot fail to be delighted by the beautiful birthday cake depicting one of the best-loved and most heroic operatic figures – Madame Butterfly. Sculpting a cake in the form of a figure can be difficult if you try to reproduce the proportions of the human body. Although nature has cleverly arranged that the weight of the body can be carried easily on slender legs, a cake cannot be top heavy and still stand erect. To solve the problem you must either design the limbs in particular ways that give greater balance or, as in this instance, clothe the body in a manner that gives weight to the base of the design. Madame Butterfly, swathed in a gorgeous kimono and cape, provides a perfect subject for interpretation in fully edible materials. Although the finished cake appears very elaborate and stunning, it is quite easy to make involving simple processes of carving and modelling the basic form, after which the lavish effect of the design is gradually built up with several layers of icing.

FOR THE MADAME BUTTERFLY CAKE

two each 8in (20cm) and 6in (15cm) round cakes
2lb (900g) marzipan
sieved apricot jam
doll's head (for mould)
1lb (450g) gelatin icing
1lb (450g) fondant icing
food colours: red, yellow, blue, green, flesh pink, pink, black, gold, silver
seed and drop pearls
cocktail sticks
small dried flowers
paper parasol

THE CAKE

The basis of the design is two 8in (20cm) and two deep 6in (15cm) round cakes. These are initially carved to create the general contours of the clothed figure. The detail is then built up in layers, first with marzipan and then with gelatin icing. The head of the figure is separately moulded out of gelatin icing.

Carving the cake

The carving process is quite simple, as you are aiming only to give a general shape to the body and clothing of the figure. If in doubt, it is as well to proceed in small steps until you have a satisfactory effect. Refer to the pictures on the previous page before you begin, to get a clear sense of what you are aiming for.

1 Stack the cakes one on top of another, with the two 8in (20cm) cakes forming the base of the stack and the two 6in (15cm) cakes on top aligned vertically at one side. The vertical side of the stack is the front of the cake where you will carve the body of the figure. The "stepped" back of the cake will form the cape trailing behind the figure.

2 With a sharp knife carve a vertical line down the front edge of the cake to a depth of about 1/2in (1.2cm). Then from a point about 1 1/2in (4cm) away from the top of the first line, carve another line from top to bottom of the cake stack. These two lines mark the body of the figure.

3 On one side of the cake, cut vertically through the cake stack at right angles to the first line, taking out a narrow triangular wedge of cake. Repeat on the other side, cutting at right angles to the second line. This leaves a "column" of cake standing proud at the front, flanked by cutaway triangular "wings".

4 To shape the cape, make a series of sloping cuts from the shoulder area down to the back edge of the cake. To begin with, position your knife at a point about 1in (2.5cm) behind the body piece that you have just carved. Cut a gentle, sweeping curve from the starting point down to the back edge of the bottom cake in the stack.

5 In the same way, make a series of curves all around the back of the cake to model the sweep of the cape behind the body. It doesn't matter if the shape is rather rough-looking at this stage, as it will be refined when you cover the cake with layers of marzipan and icing.

Marzipanning the cake

In this design, marzipan is used to cover and seal the cake in the usual way, but also to model parts of the figure to give it depth and movement. It is not necessary to achieve any realistic detail in the modelling of the limbs, as these will be mainly covered by clothing applied in subsequent layers, but they do contribute to a more natural impression in the finished figure.

In our example, the carved cake is about 10in (25cm) high and we used about 2lb (900g) marzipan in total. The covering layer of marzipan is applied in two sections, first to the cape, then to the body.

1 Spread sieved apricot jam across the back and sides of the cake, the section forming the cape. Roll out about 1 1/2lb (675g) marzipan into a sheet about 1/4in (6mm) thick. Drape the sheet of marzipan over the back of the cake and trim it to the cake base. Gently shape the marzipan to the shoulders of the figure and trim it to the edges of the body.

2 Apply sieved apricot jam to the front of the cake, that is, the protruding section forming the figure's body. Roll out the remaining marzipan to a sheet about 1/4in (6mm) thick and drape this over the front of the cake, moulding it to the sides of the body. Trim the edges where they meet the marzipan covering the back section of the cake.

3 To model the arms, roll out a piece of marzipan to pencil thickness and cut two pieces about 2-2 1/2in (5-6cm) in length. Fix each piece in turn to the front of the cake at the top, using a little apricot jam to secure them. Bring the pieces round on the front of the cake at about mid-height and fix them in place with one arm slightly above the other.

4 Cut two slightly elongated triangles of marzipan with the longest edge measuring about 1½in (4cm). Round off the edges of the triangles and fix them underneath the arms, like long sleeves trailing downward.

5 Roll out a piece of marzipan to pencil thickness and cut a 2in (5cm) length. Stick this to the body of the figure at one side to represent one leg coming forward from the body.

Modelling the head
Ideally, the face of Madame Butterfly should be quite fine and detailed, but we wanted to find a way of creating this image without a long and laborious process of modelling the head with crafting tools. The simplest way to achieve this is to take a mould from a doll's face using gelatin icing.
We happened to have a delicate porcelain doll that was the perfect model and it featured a ceramic cap that gave us the basic shape of the hairline within the same mould. However, if you work from a doll that has hair, simply make the icing mould over the face, neck and chest of the doll, then fill out the head with soft icing as explained below.
To begin with, make up 1lb (450g) gelatin icing. You only need a small piece to model the face and neck, but the rest will be used in the later stages when you model the clothing on the figure.

1 On a work surface dusted with cornflour, roll out a piece of gelatin icing as thinly as possible. Gently lay the icing over the face, neck and chest of the doll and lightly press it over all the important detail.

2 Using a sharp knife, trim the icing around the face, down the sides of the neck and onto part of the chest. Allow the icing to dry for at least 12 hours.

3 Remove the hardened icing from the doll's face. Make a ball of soft icing and press it gently into the face from behind. Ease it out around the hairline to form the overall shape of the head.

4 When the head is complete, fix it to the body of the cake, filling any gaps between the neck and shoulders with marzipan. Allow the marzipan to dry for about one hour. It doesn't matter if the junction of neck and shoulders is imperfectly modelled, as this will be covered with icing layers during the next stage.

Creating the icing layers
The process of icing this cake is not a simple matter of covering the shape with icing, but applying it in layers to represent all the layers of clothing in traditional Japaneses costume. This has the advantage that any imperfections in each icing layer can be covered or disguised by the next. Only the final layer needs to be as clean and accurate as possible. We recommend that you use gelatin icing for clothing the body, as it can be rolled out very thinly and holds very sharp lines when it is cut and arranged, so that the effect is really like beautifully draped and folded fabric. However, gelatin icing is brittle when dry and, if used for the entire cake, is likely to fracture when the cake is cut. You might prefer to use the crispness of gelatin icing for modelling detail in the front part of the figure but to apply fondant icing to the cape, making it easier to cut the main portion. This does not quite have the fineness of gelatin icing when it comes to creating dramatic detail.

1 Take the gelatin icing left over from making the head and roll it out into a thin sheet. Cut two rectangles about 4 × ½in (10 × 1.2cm). Drape these in turn around the neck of the figure, bringing one over the other at the front to form a V-shaped collar. Fix them onto the chest by dampening the underlying marzipan layer with a little clean water.

2 To create the drapery of the kimono below the arms, first brush the lower part of the figure with water to moisten the marzipan and make it tacky. Roll out the gelatin icing thinly and stick the icing sheet to the front of the cake. Trim it to the sides of the body and underneath the sleeves.

3 Gather up the remaining icing and roll it out thinly again. Cut two rectangles 4 × 1½in (10 × 4cm). Starting under the arms, arrange each of these pieces to fall downwards, parting at knee level so that the leg coming forward is just revealed. These two rectangles form the kimono painted red in the finished picture.

4 To make the sash, cut a rectangle of icing about ½in (1.2cm) wide and 2in (5cm) long. Moistening the underlayer with a little water, fix this just underneath the arms, slightly covering the sleeves. Trim the edges to shape.

5 To form the drapery coloured blue in the finished picture, cut two rectangles of icing about 12 × 1½in (30 × 4cm). Fix each piece behind the head and bring them down the front of the figure, leaving the hands and the front of the kimono exposed.

6 To create the cape, first make a template for the shape so that you will not have to trim the icing once it is applied to the cake. Use a piece of tissue paper or fine fabric for the template. Drape it over the back of the cake and mark the lines of the cape with food colour pen or other marker. Remove the paper or fabric and cut out the shape. Use this as a pattern to cut the sheet of icing. Moisten the marzipan on the back of the cake with water and apply the icing.

Colour decoration
Painting with food colours over the white icing gives the most vibrant effect of colour and tone. The designs that we have applied to the layers of clothing were taken from greeting cards and wrapping papers decorated on oriental themes. The white base of the kimono carries a delicate design of small butterflies painted in gold. The next layer is a plain, rich scarlet. The third level of drapery is an oriental tree and blossom design in brilliant blue, yellow and white. The white cape is decorated with a bright and beautiful chrysanthemum design surrounded by bold butterflies.
If you are confident in painting, you can draw the designs freehand on the icing using a fine paintbrush and a pale shade of food colour. Otherwise, you can draw up the motifs on greaseproof paper and score through the paper template with a cocktail stick to leave a lightly impressed outline in the icing while it is still soft. You should apply only very light pressure, otherwise parts of the icing that are not supported by the cake may break.

Finishing touches.
The final step is to add detail to the head and face. The face remains virtually white, with only a very light blush of flesh tint. The eyebrows and eyes are painted with thin lines of black and the mouth with red. The hair is solid black.
The headdress consists of a few individual seed pearls stuck to the head with tiny dabs of royal icing, two drop pearls arranged to the side and some tiny individual dried flowers. The sticks characteristic of the hairstyle that goes with the formal Japanese gown are pieces of cocktail sticks coloured with food colour and attached to the head with a little royal icing. Icing used to secure the headdress can be painted black to blend into the hair.

113

CHAPTER 9

SETTING THE SCENE

Whether your celebration is arranged for one special guest or for everyone you know, the mood and setting can be as important to the success of the occasion as the food that you serve. In this section, we suggest a range of ideas for creating the right atmosphere and we begin with the essential mood-maker – the lighting. Everyone loves the intimacy and warmth of candlelight but our designs add to its special presence by gently shading the light in decorative and unexpected ways: It is usual for a buffet or dinner party table to have a centrepiece, often an elaborate floral design that is, for all its beauty, merely decorative. We have suggested thinking of the centrepiece rather as a sculpture for the table that can be constructed from materials you already have. Look around your kitchen and you will find many things to inspire you. Stencils are a quick and easy way to add colour and pattern to papers, fabrics and cakes. Whether you wish to decorate the whole room or some of the items in it, stencilling helps you to coordinate your ideas.

CANDLE SHADES

These individual designs are all based on a single rectangle of paper or cardboard rolled into a tube. The most basic of the designs consists only of a rolled piece of parchment-like paper (foreground right) that softly disperses the candlelight. Two variations on this theme (left) include simple decorative bands at top and bottom of the shade, while in the gold-paper shade (foreground left), the pattern is cut into the paper, making facets of light. The fan is an elegant idea for redirecting the soft light of the candle standing behind it. This, too, can be made from a paper rectangle, or you can use a bought fan. A candle holder with its own shade (far right) is given a different appearance to suit the mood with a decorative paper shade slipped over the original.

WOODLAND SHADE

An arrangement of natural objects – twigs, cones, dried and fresh flowers – has a particular charm whem illuminated from the inside. A glass tumbler covers the candle at the centre of the design, protecting the components of the arrangement from the flame. The centrepiece of this arrangement can be kept as a permanent decoration, with additional elements introduced according to the season or the mood of the occasion.

GOLDEN LILIES

Beautiful white and green paper lilies glow warmly with individual candles set within each flower. The process of making the tall lilies is quite simple but the effect is elegant and unusual. The candle holder is made from a circle of wire with twisted ends (top right) and attached to a dowel. The lily and leaves are cut from paper and coloured (centre right), then foided into shape and slipped over the candle holder. The lily is secured and the dowel disguised with green florists' tape (bottom right).

Making the lilies *(right) Make the candle holders for the lily centres by attaching a ring of wire, shaped to fit the candle, to a length of wood dowelling. Twist the ends of wire to secure the loop and bind them to the dowelling with strong thread.*

Trace the shapes of the lily petal and leaves on textured paper and cut them to shape. Colour the base of the flower and the leaves with green paint and leave them to dry.

Form the lily petal into a cone and slot the candle holder into the centre. Bind the base of the lily to the dowelling with florists' tape, at the same time attaching a leaf to the stem below the flower.

LIGHT AND MOOD

There can be few more pleasing sights in a room than the mellow light and soft shadows created by the flare of candles. Certainly there are few simpler ways of creating atmosphere.
In this section, we have concentrated on simple but effective ways of making the most of this beautiful form of natural light and enhancing its presence.
The instructions for recreating our designs must be preceded by a word of warning. While candlelight is exceptionally beautiful, there is always some danger in a naked flame. Any kind of shade that you create for a candle has the potential to burn, therefore you must always construct the shade with plenty of space between the fabric or paper and the flame, so there is no intense or direct contact with the source of heat. And however well considered your decorations, never leave a room unattended when there are candles burning.

CANDLE SHADES

All the candle shades illustrated are based on using a rectangle of cardboard or stiff paper and finding very simple ways of making the basic material a little more decorative. Each of the tube-shaped shades is freestanding with the candle at the centre, so make sure your original rectangle forms a large enough tube to keep the sides well clear of the flame.

1 The first design is made of a heavy, cream paper with a veined parchment texture, which emphasizes the golden colour of the candlelight shining through. All you need to do is cut a rectangle of paper, curve it and join the two sides into a single seam, secured with double-sided adhesive tape.

2 The second design is a variation on the first. Before joining the rectangle into a tube, add 1in (2.5cm) wide strips of the same paper, glued to the top and bottom edges of the rectangle. When secured as before, the shade has its own slightly shadowed effect at the top and base.

3 For the third design, leave a margin of about ½in (1.2cm) at top and bottom of the rectangle and from this margin cut vertical slits in the paper about ½in (1.2cm) deep and at intervals of about 2in (5cm). Thread metallic ribbon or strips of paper through the slits before closing up the tube as before.

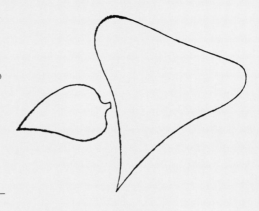

greaseproof paper and tape the edges of the paper together. Lift the paper cover off the shade, cut it from top to bottom and open it out. This gives you a pattern for cutting a new shade from a different material. When tracing your pattern onto the selected paper, add an extra ½in (1.2cm) at one end to allow an overlap where you can secure the edges. Decorate the paper shade in any way appropriate to the occasion and slip it over the existing shade. (Note that the double thickness will cut down the amount of transmitted light.)

WOODLAND SHADE

An unusual and very beautiful effect comes from incorporating the light source, in this case a nightlight, within an arrangement of dried and fresh flowers, twigs and other natural objects, offset with a large ribbon bow. The objects can be collected from woodland, garden or park.

The centre of the piece is a glass tumbler wrapped in brown paper secured with adhesive tape. Using strong adhesive, stick twigs and stems around the wrapped glass, creating a graded effect with smaller stems at the front rising to larger, heavier twigs at the back. Then wrap the ribbon around the twigs and tie it in a decorative bow.

Place the tumbler over the nightlight to create a subdued glow. Arrange other natural items around the decorated centre – nuts, mosses, pinecones, evergreen leaf sprays – and finish by arranging a few dried and fresh flowers in association with the twigs.

GOLDEN LILIES

This design creates a particularly spectacular effect since the candlelight actually emerges from the cups of the white paper arum lilies, creating strong individual shapes with a golden glow. The lilies are attached to stems made of lengths of dowelling. To give an elegant, natural appearance, make the stems tall but slightly different in height. Since the tallness may make the lilies top-heavy, the base of the completed arrangement should be weighted or secured to avoid accident.

1 Trace and enlarge the pattern for the lily shape. As a guide to size, in the example shown the lily heads measure 6-8in (15-20cm) from tip to base. Transfer the outline to textured paper and cut three flower shapes. At the same time, cut three rounded leaves and three slender strap-shaped leaves from the same paper.

4 The fourth example is again based on a rectangle, but cut to form a decorative pierced effect. Having cut the rectangle (we have used a textured gold paper), draw a grid of 1in (2.5cm) squares on the wrong side. Using a sharp scalpel, cut along the diagonals of every alternate square and push the cut shapes outwards. Then simply roll the rectangle into a tube and secure with double-sided tape.

5 The next design is slightly more ambitious in that the rectangle of paper is formed into a fan (you can of course use a bought paper fan if you prefer). To make a fan, simply pleat a long rectangle of paper by making folds in alternate directions at regular intervals. Fold the pleated strip in half and hold the folded end in one hand. With the other hand, open out the pleats to form the fan shape. Secure the centre join between the two halves of the fan with adhesive or double-sided tape.

To create a secure base on which the opened fan can rest upright, fix the lower edge of the opened fan to a wooden rod or lath about 1in (2.5cm) wide. Set the fan in front of the candle.

6 The final design is a paper shade decorated with metallic cord, which is mounted on a holder that supports both candle and shade. If you have a holder of this type you can adapt the design of the existing shade, enabling you to create a decorative effect in keeping with the theme or atmosphere of the particular occasion.

Wrap the original shade snugly in

2 Colour the leaves and the base of the flower with green paint. Use a sponge or spray to apply the colour delicately. Leave them to dry.

3 Make candle holders for each of the flowers as follows. Take a nightlight or a short length of white candle and a length of wire about 8in (20cm) long. Hold the candle at the centre of the wire and wrap the wire once around the candle. Twist the ends of wire together. Release the circle of wire from the candle and bend the twisted ends down at right angles to it.

4 For each candle holder, cut a piece of ¼in (6mm) dowelling about 30in (75cm) long. Bind the twisted end of the candle holder to one end of the dowelling, using strong thread. Make sure the binding is very secure. Refit the candle to the holder.

5 Take the paper shape for each flower and twist it into a cone with the edges overlapping. Secure the seam with adhesive or double-sided tape. Push the dowelling down through the centre of the flower and ease the flower up the stem so that the candle holder sits at the centre of the flower.

6 Bind the base of the flower with florists' tape and use the tape to secure it to the dowelling. After two or three turns, attach the rounded leaf below the flower base and tape it in place. Continue to wrap the dowelling with tape to about two-thirds of its length. Then attach the strap-like leaf and tape it in position. Finish taping to the end of the stem.

7 Make the base of the arrangment from a block of dry florists' foam mounted on a piece of thick card or lightweight wood. Push the lily stems into the foam block and disguise the base by covering it with short-stemmed dried Chinese lanterns.

117

TABLE SCULPTURES

Each of these dramatically impressive still lifes is based on the simple principle of using items that are already in your kitchen or that have some practical as well as decorative use. This extends to incorporating edible components that contribute to the menu of your dinner party or buffet table. Fresh breads and fruits are naturally attractive items and the idea is simply to create a sumptuous mass of the edibles, sympathetically arranged with the most attractive of your kitchen containers – pans, dishes, bottles, moulds, baskets. The designs combine the wholesome atmosphere and charm of the country kitchen with an elegance that would not be out of place in a more formal setting. Unlike the complex flower arrangements so often used for table centrepieces, which can be very daunting if you do not have skill or flair for that kind of decorative work, the still lifes suggest their own colour schemes and depend upon the inherently sculptural qualities of the components to create a pleasing arrangement of form and texture.

119

CENTREPIECES — TABLE SCULPTURES

Creating the centrepiece of a dinner party or buffet table can be a daunting prospect, usually because most people think of complex flower arrangements that require particular skills and techniques and hours of painstaking work. In fact, it can be easier than you think to create a beautiful focal point using flowers. You might select a single type of flower with a natural grace and elegance, tulips, for example, and simply mass several bunches in a well-shaped glass vase, allowing the flowers to speak for themselves.

In our designs for table centres, we have taken an entirely different approach from the traditional style of flower display. Each design calls into play ordinary items that may already be available in your own kitchen and basic foods that contribute their own beauty and character to the design. Using these everyday objects, you can create innovative sculptural forms that easily rival the most elaborate flower arrangement.

—BEAUTIFUL BREADS—

Our first example demonstrates the visual potential of one of the most simple and inexpensive foods. We have chosen a wide variety of breads, with a range of colours, shapes and textures, and have chosen to offset them against a large copper bowl. The bowl creates a frame for the design and its burnished copper tones are a superbly rich background to the colours and textures of the breads. To create the variations of shape and colour, we have selected plaited and crescent loaves, bread sticks, twists and rolls. These are simply piled together, grading outwards from the interior of the bowl, arranged to create an interesting and balanced design relying on the natural harmony of the ingredients. One of the bread sticks is torn to release the freshness of the soft interior and add the contrast of a rough textural quality.

To complement the rich tones of gold and brown, we have placed within the design small terracotta pots filled with dried flowers. Ivy stems lazily wound into the bread stack create colour contrast and complete the rustic charm of this piece. There is, of course, the advantage that this decoration can form part of the meal and is especially suitable for a large buffet table. You could add attractive

waxed corks and calligraphic lettering on the sides. The overall effect of the design is a very pleasing combination of planes and colours with a clean sculptural quality.

As with the breads, this centrepiece is quite large, so depending on the size of your table and what it has to accommodate, you might wish to adapt the design using fewer components. You could also convert the idea for a simple flower arrangement using, perhaps, large flowerheads such as hydrangeas in association with simple but elegant ceramic containers.

An alternative interpretation, if you have no suitable moulds or bottles to create the sculptured form, is to create a pyramid of lemons on top of a plain glass or white china cake stand. This can be given a twining garland of ivy to add to the freshness and crispness of the colours. A particularly beautiful effect comes from brushing the ivy leaves lightly with oil to make them glisten among the fruits. For a long buffet table, you could make two such pyramids, one for either end, and continue the colour themes throughout the decoration of the table, using cool white and fresh spring colours.

—BASKET OF APPLES—

The final design for a table sculpture concentrates on the juxtapositions of shape, colour and texture in the shining red apples and rustic basket. The basket is made of wicker and fibre and has a piece of sacking threaded into leather thongs around the top, in itself an interesting arrangement of elements. The apples were chosen for their good colouring, with some green pointing up the rich reds, and blemish-free shapes and textures. We simply polished them to a high shine and massed them in the basket, then as a finishing touch added some twining ivy leaves.

This is a basic idea that has great versatility. You can give an entirely different character to the design according to the kind of fruit you select. Apricots would bring the bonus of their delicious perfume, and the bloom on the golden skins would make a wonderful focus of light in a table centre. You might add pretty flowers and leaf sprays to set off the fruit. Alternatively, you could use a decorative bowl as the container for a mass of plump cherries, perhaps adding ice cubes and a light spray of water to create a cool, glistening, jewel-like effect. Once you realize how simple the components of a stunning centrepiece can be, there is no end to the possibilities.

cheeses, biscuits and fruits, extending the arrangement down the centre of a long table so that it makes a substantial contribution to the foods in the buffet as well as a highly decorative feature of the full table setting.

—STILL LIFE WITH— LEMONS

For the second design, we have used pieces of cream and white pottery and porcelain that were readily available in the kitchen. These include antique jelly moulds with decoratively fluted interiors. If you have a strong interest in cookery you may have acquired similar beautiful but practical items, but any simple and attractively designed ceramic ware can be used to create a still life for a table centre.

Two of the moulds are placed on their sides to feature the decorative interior, the other two are upturned and filled with beautiful plump, clear lemons. As a complement to the yellow fruit, sprays of tiny purple flowers form a charming contrast.

The design is completed with two ceramic bottles. These have gentle outlines and provide additional visual interest in the

STENCILLED CAKE

Stencils are easy to make and give you great versatility in cake decoration. This basic stencil design of a fruit and leaf pattern has a fresh, clean effect and could look very different painted in other colourways. You can use a single stencil cut with the entire design, or stencils of individual motifs that can be repeated around the cake. If your design means that you will need to move the stencil to repeat the pattern, it is best to make it initially from clear acetate so that you can see through it to position it in relation to colours you have already applied.

Applying colour *Hold your stencil on the iced cake and dab food colour into the exposed areas with a brush.*

An easy alternative to making your own stencil is to use a paper doily with a precut design and select various areas to receive different colours.

122

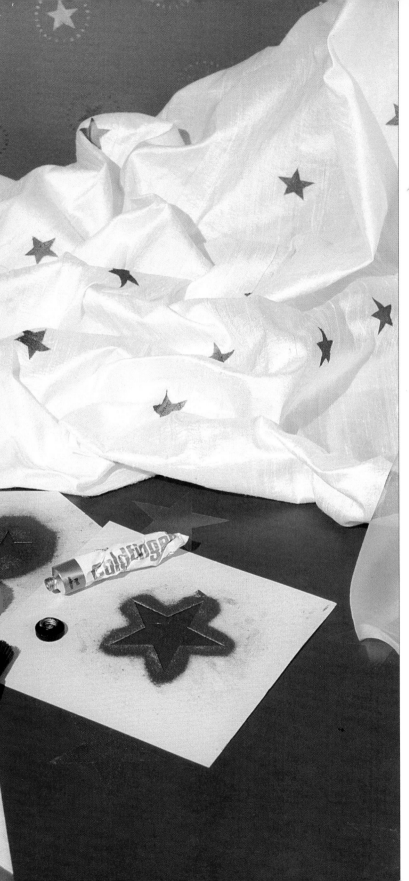

STENCILLING ON PAPER AND FABRIC

All sorts of finishes can be applied to paper using paint colours with the traditional stencil brush (above) or using spray paints or markers. Special colours are available for use on fabric, which will not wash out. In this way you can apply a motif appropriate to the party theme to every item of your decoration. The simplest form of stencil is a whole shape cut out of the centre of a piece of cardboard or acetate. These examples show how a large and a small star create basic all-over repeat patterns or borders for paper and fabric. The medium used for these papers was finger gold, a product made for adding colour and texture to gilded picture frames. It is available in a wide range of shades of gold.

STENCILLED PATTERNS

Stencilling is a very easy and attractive way of carrying a theme through every aspect of your decorations for a party or celebration. You can create an image with stencils and apply it to gift wrappings, name and menu cards, napkins, tablecloths and place mats, and even lampshades. You can also apply stencilling to decorate your cake. All sorts of items quickly become part of a beautifully devised decorative scheme that can be composed of any shapes and colours that you like. You can use pre-cut stencils, available from department stores and suppliers of paper products, but you can also easily draw and cut your own stencils to give a specially personal touch to the design.

Stencilling materials

The best material for making stencils is clear acetate in sheet form. This is available in varying thicknesses as standard-sized sheets or off the roll. It is quite durable and can be washed down to remove traces of colour without any damage to the edges and corners of the stencil. Because you can see through it, it is especially useful if you are going to make a stencil pattern that involves repeating or overlaying the motifs. You can locate an acetate stencil accurately on a half-completed design.

The alternative material is cardboard, preferably of good quality. A cardboard stencil that is used repeatedly should be treated beforehand to make it resistant to the wet colour, otherwise it will become damp and the edges are likely to fray. Draw the design onto the cardboard before you treat it, as the treated surface is oily and resistant to drawing materials. Mix a solution of one part linseed oil to one part turpentine, rub the liquid over the card and leave it to dry.

If you are using the stencil in the traditional manner, you will require at least one stencil brush. This has a head of stiff bristles cut flat across the top. It is worth buying the best quality that you can afford, as this does tend to be reflected in the end result. A stencil brush will last a long time with proper care – always clean it thoroughly between colour applications and when you finish using it.

You will also need a scalpel or fine craft knife, with a supply of blades so that you can replace the blade as soon as it becomes blunted. Use the type of straight-edged blade that slants to a point, rather than the rounded blades also sold for these knives.

Colours for stencilling are available for using on both paper and fabric. Fabric colours can be obtained from artists' suppliers, specialist stencil shops or some large department stores. There is a wide range of colours and they will survive the washing process. For stencilling on paper you can use stencil colours or select from the huge range of paints and colour finishes, and you don't have to use a traditional stencil brush – markers, for example, are quick and easy to use with stencils.

Designing stencils

If you are making stencils to your own design, you can use one of two basic forms. The simplest stencil consists of a shape cut out of the acetate or card and the colour is applied across the whole of the cut-out shape. Simple stencils can be used singly, as we have done to create the repeat star pattern on the papers and fabrics shown in the photograph. Or you can combine individual shapes, stencilled with different colours to build a more complex design, as with our cake.

In the second kind of stencil, the final impression of the image depends on the dual effect of colour applied through the exposed areas combined with the impression left in the areas not touched with colour. For example, in a stencil of a rose, because of the complexity of the flower shape, what is not coloured is as important as the coloured sections in the final effect.

Stencil patterns can be as simple or as complex as you wish, but when you begin to design your own it is probably as well to keep them fairly simple. This applies to the number of colours as well as the shapes. Too many colours can be rather messy to apply and the design can look over-complex. You can very simply create additional detail and depth in the design by stencilling a darker shade over a light one or, in some cases, a second colour over the first.

Colour application

The method you use for colouring the stencil pattern depends on the medium you use. Stencil brushes are used with liquid and powder colour, as described

below. Alternatively, it is extremely quick and easy to apply colour as a spray, using an airbrush or a mist-sprayer. You simply hold the stencil in place and spray the exposed areas in one swift movement.

1 Position the stencil on the surface of the fabric or paper and hold it in place. You may wish to tape it down to prevent any movement, especially if you intend to add further colour to the same areas.

2 Mix the paint or powder colour in a saucer and dip the stencil brush lightly into the paint so that the bristles are not overloaded with colour. Blot the brush tip gently on a piece of tissue or kitchen paper.

3 Apply colour to the exposed area of the stencil with a light dabbing motion, gradually building the strength of colour over the whole area. If you are going to overlay colours one on another, leave the first application fairly light.

4 Move the stencil to the next position and repeat the process. Work one colour at a time and allow it to dry before overlaying other tones or hues.

Metallic finishes for papers

If you are stencilling on paper, for use as wrapping paper or party decoration such as temporary lampshade covers, you can use metallic powders in association with a light spray varnish. This method is unsuitable for fabrics or edible products.

1 Position the stencil on the paper, secured with tape if necessary. Spray the exposed areas with varnish.

2 Before the varnish dries, while the surface is still tacky, dab on the metallic powder. The best way to do this is to wrap your forefinger in a clean cloth, dab the cloth in the powder and then apply it to the varnish area.

FOR THE STENCILLED CAKE

round cake, marzipanned and iced

acetate or card stencil

food colours as required

stencilling brush

THE CAKE

Stencilling a cake

Our example shows a very attractive repeat pattern in three colours applied with food colour over fondant icing. For this we have used a hand-cut stencil. It is important to allow the fondant icing time to dry before you start stencilling. Otherwise the stencil may stick to the cake, or the colours may spread under the stencil, creating an indistinct image.

1 To begin with, simply marzipan and ice your cake in the usual way. Allow the fondant icing to dry for about eight hours before beginning the stencilling.

2 Cut the stencil to fit the size of the cake and mix up the required food colours. Load the brush with colour and blot off the excess. Apply the first colour to the appropriate sections of the stencil and allow it to dry.

3 Repeat the process to add the second and third colours. When all the colour is dry, you can add detail in the form of highlights or colour shading if you wish. As an alternative to cutting your own stencil, you can decorate a cake using a paper doily as the stencil. This gives quite a detailed, delicate effect. To keep the doily in place while you apply the colours, simply pin it to the icing layer. Remember to remove all of the pins when the work is completed.

125

Taurus

Gemini

Spring Violet

ACKNOWLEDGEMENTS

Greg Robinson and Max Schofield would like to thank Judy Martin for her excellent work in editing the book and Matthew Chattle for his superb photography and enthusiasm, particular thanks to Sally Stockwell and Nigel Osborne for their hard work and enormous patience, and sense of style. Greg and Max would also like to thank Glynn Christian for his willingness to offer guidance, encouragement and most importantly his friendship.